What About Us?

Tales from an Angry Mass Transit Bus Operator

C. C. Wurld

AuthorHouse™
1663 Liberty Drive
Bloomington, IN 47403
www.authorhouse.com
Phone: 1-800-839-8640

First published by AuthorHouse 09/13/2011

ISBN: 978-1-4634-1516-7 (sc)
ISBN: 978-1-4634-1515-0 (ebk)

Library of Congress Control Number: 2011915053

Printed in the United States of America

This book is printed on acid-free paper.

Contents

The Streets Are a Beast

MY COWORKERS AND I, all mass transit operators in one of the largest cities in the United States, are public enemy number one. We are greatly unappreciated and get absolutely no respect from anyone, starting with management and trickling all the way down to the riders. I often ask myself, "Why in the hell am I getting dirt kicked in my face?" I honestly cannot come up with one level-headed answer for why members of the public act like fools at a drop of a dime. Violence toward transit system staff occurs every day, 24/7. This disturbing behavior is scary because it is so unpredictable, and it is far too easy for transit system operators to become victims of brutal attacks.

There is nothing to stop anyone from bashing my head onto the steering wheel, spitting in my face, throwing rocks and bottles, stabbing me in my chest, wrapping their hands or a rope around my neck, licking my face, inappropriately touching my body, raping me, or even killing me. Nothing! We are in a constant battle, facing verbal abuse, the pure filth—both human waste and garbage—left by the public, and actual physical, blood-splattering fights. Transit bus and trolley operators are all alone, butt-naked in the jungle, surrounded by snakes, lions, tigers, and bears. We cry, "Help! Protect us!" to management day after day, week after week, month after month, and year after year, and still no one hears our cries. It's almost as though we have been left here to die. We are being eaten alive.

I believe that transit system operators are more likely to face gunfire than cops are. Hundreds of thousands of people travel on mass transit each day. We do not know any of these people. But there is one thing I do know: we are driving around murderers, thieves, psychopaths, pedophiles, pickpockets, rapists. You name it, we drive it. For instance, along some bus routes in our city there is a whole strip of homes and prisons where former criminals live. They have some place to get to and, guess what, they ride our vehicles. And they are dangerous! Operators, you had better watch your backs. You had better hit that help button or call in sick so that a supervisor can relieve you of your duties.

News flash! Let the truth be told, and read all about it! Most problems are not caused by these ex-felons. The bulk of my problems—the dramas, altercations, and confrontations—are with females, females, and more females. If a woman violates a rule and regulation, it is my job requirement as the enforcer to issue a warning. But because I am also female, I usually get nasty attitudes and cussed out. That is not to say that I don't have any problems with men; however, they are a low percentage.

I refuse to believe that the big city in which I live and work is the only one that experiences violence toward transit system operators. It isn't possible! Daily violence in mass transit systems has to be a worldwide problem. Think about the horrific, deadly bombings and constant threats faced by the airlines. But airlines have taken great measurements not only to protect the health, safety, and welfare of the public but also of their dedicated, hardworking employees. The laws protecting the airlines are enforced, and everyone on planet Earth knows what they are. Every airline has the same standard rules:

1. Arrive two to three hours before departure time.
2. Each passenger is allowed a limited number of carry-on bags.
3. Checked luggage may be opened and checked.
4. Passengers may be asked to comply with full-body x-rays and possibly a strip search.

Now tell me that is not a damn good evidence of management and the government stepping up and securing the lives of their employees and giving them a level of comfort and stability within their work environment.

Yet transit system operators work in this cruel world without an ounce of decent protection. They have obligations to fulfill and duties to perform. To ensure that we provide excellent service and a safe and comfortable ride, all we ask of the passengers is to obey the rules and regulations and allow us to keep clear heads, focus on the roads, and get the vehicles down the street. Are we asking too much? Is following a direct order so hard to do? It is always amazing to me that a request to a passenger can result in the transit system employee being called every foul name under God's great, big, beautiful blue sky. After years of driving a bus, I have taught myself to become immune to the name-calling. I have grown a deaf ear. Being called a bitch does not even faze me. Bitch is my name when I am behind that wheel.

However, if I get the feeling that a situation is about to get straight ignorant and flourish into an out-of-control, full-blown argument, I stop driving immediately and call my supervisor and the police. I have had to figure out how to protect myself, find sanity, and keep my peace of mind while driving this massive vehicle full of passengers eight or more hours a day. No, drivers are not looking for trouble with the passengers. And Lord knows we do not want danger coming our way. Do you know anyone who does? Nor are we trying to be jerks, as many passengers seem to believe. We have a J-O-B to do. Just because we are public servants does not mean we do not get stressed out! By way of example, I ask you to visualize a few of the many annoying questions that drive operators nuts!

It is two o'clock on a rainy afternoon; the windshield wipers move vigorously across my windows. The sky grows darker, my high beams are on, and the quality of my road vision is poor.

A passenger asks, with attitude, "Why are you driving so damn slow?"

My answer: "You've got to be kidding. I'm sorry, but are you blind?"

Passenger's response: "Bitch!"

All I can do is roll my eyes, smirk, and shake my head at the stupidity. If school buses, Mack trucks, and sixty- to seventy-foot tractor trailers slip, slide, sway side to side, and flip over in the rain, what makes a public bus any different?

It is five o'clock, in rush-hour traffic. Three to four buses displaying the same routes come down the street at the same time, each one packed front to back with passengers like sardines.

A passenger asks, with attitude, "Why are you so late? I've been waiting over an hour! This happens every day and it makes no sense!"

I stand up and announce, "It is called *rush hour*, which means there are traffic jams and delays all over the city due to people getting off from work and trying to go home just like you! Another thing, call the authorities or picket in front of their building. They have cut services, which means there are fewer mass transit vehicles on the streets to provide for the people! Yelling at me ain't going to get you anywhere. Use that energy to make changes by contacting the mass transit system authority managers."

The passenger's response: "Whatever! Bitch!"

Again, I roll my eyes, smirk, and shake my head.

I wish that daily rider would have gained some type of knowledge to answer her own simple question.

Picking up shiploads of people at every stop?
Accidents and incidents?
Traffic jams?
Broken-down vehicles?
Rush hour?

None of that seems to matter. Public transportation is unpredictable. But I do not know any operator who wants to be late at any time. We are trying to get down that street, to make it from point A to point B as promptly as we can so we can use those seven minutes at the end of our trips to use the restroom, stretch, catch our breath, and gather our thoughts. Those itsy-bitsy minutes are precious, and every little bit counts. Being a mass transit system authority operator has to rate in the top five of the most stressful and dangerous jobs in the world. We have the highest volume of face-to-face customer interactions, without any assistance from on-the-spot management, and often have to defend ourselves and handle the situation immediately. Protection or help from management usually comes later. Many of the times, to try and make people understand our points of view, we must make decisions ourselves using common sense, the knowledge of the business, a God-given strength for tolerance, and the belief that there is someone out there having worse day than we are. Aye, that is just the way it is. If you do not have a good home base or any outside activities other than the job, you will go crazy. This job will make you hate people, a feeling that a few of my coworkers have shared with me. Others develop medical problems or have nervous breakdowns: you become jumpy, everything scares you, and everyone irks you. Some drivers become hooked on medications just to get them through the day. The streets are a beast.

Most riders are entirely clueless about what operators have to deal with. Most seem to believe that I'm tooting my own horn and blowing smoke out of my ass. I have been told to my face that a five-year-old child could do my job. "All y'all do is drive up and down these streets without any type of pressures. Who can't do that?" Think about those statements. Now question yourself, and reminisce about back in the day when you learned how to roller skate, skate board, or ride a bike. A broken nose, scraped knees, or an aching body likely made you realize that the only way to be good at what you set out to do is to *concentrate*. You must employ all your mental powers and give your exclusive attention to the thing you want to accomplish.

Transit system operators work under pressure and in stressful conditions. We do not make any of the rules. We have bosses. Instructions for how to deal with the public come directly from management. The managers are the culprits who are hiking up the fares and cutting services. Transit system operators have to abide with these rules and regulations because it is our job to do so. Still, I know, as do my coworkers, we will continue to be threatened, harassed, and assaulted for enforcing those rules and regulations. Until management shows it is concerned about operators' lives and believes that we are worthy of having a decent work environment, violent actions against us will increase. We are not machines operating these massive vehicles. We have families who love us and care for our well-being just like everyone else. We cherish our loved ones and share our lives with them. We also are grandmothers, grandfathers, mothers, fathers, sisters, brothers, children, aunts, uncles, cousins, nieces, nephews, husbands, wives, pet owners, and friends. We know right from wrong; we've been happy and sad. We have feelings, make decisions, and have choices.

I have a heart that my God, Lord, and Savior knows.
I have a brain that allows me to use my senses, to learn, think, and make life choices.
Before I leave for work, I kiss and hug my son and wish him well every day and night. Heck, I hug, kiss, and rub my dog as well.
I laugh.
I dance.

What About Us?

I love to eat seafood, hoagies, fresh fruits, nuts, and chocolate-covered strawberries.

I gain weight.

I gain more weight.

I lose a few pounds.

I am ticklish.

I cough.

I sneeze.

I sweat when it is hot.

I shiver when it is cold.

I am tired; I yawn and pull the sheet over me.

THE PUBLIC DOES not appreciate our true qualities or that transit system operators are real-life superheroes. We are the Wonder Women, Supermen, and Batmen in the city, going strong despite all the brutality toward us, operating these large vehicles, and providing nonstop services around the clock. Like flies at a picnic, we are everywhere. You see us more than you see the police. We are in every neighborhood, from the major roads to the tiny streets—urban, suburban, river to river, on the expressways, north, south, east, and west. You can find mass transit operators working early in the morning before the rooster's cock-a-doodle-do, mid-morning, late morning, lunchtime, late afternoon, evening, nighttime, midnight. The hell with inclement weather—snow, rain, sleet, hail, and ice—the transit system management does not know what that is.

You say what? A fireball came from the sky struck a car and exploded! Poles and power lines are falling down all over the city? Lightning is striking trees up here and over there? Girl, it looks like the California wildfires. My cool response will be, "Oh just calm down, sip on some hot tea, and relax. So what if a few trees caught on fire, and there are animals, cars, and people floating in the streets due to the overflowing river. It is just an electrical rainstorm. Buses, trolleys, and trains can drive through all that! We can't be stopped." What is happening now? You say there is sixty feet of snow, hail as big as watermelons, and ice like glaciers? And again my cool response will be, "Ain't nothing stopping us, not even Mother Nature. We will be out there no matter what. Our vehicles are too large, too strong, and have tires as huge as elephants; they can withstand any weather."

Flash alert: ice is slippery, dangerous, and guaranteed to cause major traffic delays, terrible accidents, and death. If the airlines can shut down during an ice storm, why can't public buses, trolleys, and trains? Transit system vehicles can slip, slide, jack knife, and get stuck just like all the other vehicles on the roads. Transit system operators as well as passengers can become stranded and abandoned for long hours without food, restrooms, or heat. The vehicles finally give up and break down after battling brutal and unbearable weather conditions. I have been blessed by and give unconditional thanks to those restaurants, stores, and families who have expressed major concerns for my life and have invited me into their establishments and homes to get warm, eat something, and use the restrooms. Furthermore, transit system employees have to find a way to get to work ourselves. How do we get there in inclement weather? Yes, we drive our own vehicles. The transit system does not provide transportation for its employees. We are civilians, everyday people who are putting our lives in jeopardy, driving in nasty weather conditions to arrive to work, where we either sit in the depot all day or tackle the horrible weather conditions and risk putting more lives in danger. Well, at least the transit system authorities have gotten their money.

It does not matter how many times my parents, family, friends, and neighbors beg me not to go to work, worried about my safety, listening to what the local news stations are reporting: that all vehicles, including commercial vehicles, should stay off the roads due to the hazardous conditions. Unless the city has been shut down and placed in a state of emergency—i.e., everyone must stay inside with no vehicles on the road—the transit system will be open for business. Why after so many years of extensive news coverage of disabled vehicles, hundreds of accidents, and passengers and operators stranded and abandoned do administrations not realize that during disastrous weather conditions transit systems must shut down? What will it take to keep buses and trolleys off the streets? A hundred vehicles crashing into the transit system authority main building? Thousands of dead frozen bodies in the vehicles? How much destruction is enough?

Hello! I'm yelling upstairs to the "brains." Do you hear me? Oh, I forgot. The brains will not be affected by this disaster. They will be across the street at a five-star hotel, partying with the $300-million-plus that was stolen from the employees' pension plan. The only response that the transit authority administration issued was that the $300 million–plus had been "lost," and they had "no clue" as to how it disappeared. What? That had to be a joke! I was totally outraged that the managers could in effect drop their pants, bend over, and tell the employees to kiss their asses in front of the cameras from the local news stations. Unbelievable! In today's computer- and technology-savvy world, that sort of a response is disgraceful, weak, and unacceptable.

Weeks later, the managers issued a final statement regarding the pension plan: "We put the money into a money market account, hoping to double it, but we lost it all." It took them weeks to come up with that lame excuse! Now what? Are we to believe that you were actually working for the employees' benefit? Are we supposed to feel grateful because you hoped to double our hard-earned money, even though you gambled with it without asking us? There were no handouts, no brochures, no newsletters, no pamphlets, no meetings, no mailed letters, nothing posted in the depots informing us what they wanted to do with our pension plan money. Who gave them that right? Show me the proof that enables management to dig into our pockets anytime without asking. The sick part about it all is that management wants the employees to pay all of the money back!

It is the employees who keep the city alive, up and running, and always bring in a big, daily cash flow. The pension plan money was our money, not theirs. In my opinion, the transit system managers are criminals, guilty of theft. They have robbed us of millions of our hard-earned dollars, in effect our handmade diamonds and pearls.

They are a bunch of liars, who should rot in hell. I suspect they used our pension plan money for their personal gain, needs, and enjoyment: big raises; huge bonuses; flying first class; vacations with family and friends to luxurious islands and on cruises; sleeping in five-star hotels, dining at the world's best restaurants; dropping twenty grand a night; buying priceless jewelry, top-of-the-line, name-brand clothing, beautiful homes, lavish cars, fast boats, yachts, helicopters, horses, donkeys, and ponies; paid-off major bills; set up college funds; increased their retirement accounts. They were living like multimillionaires. And the most disgusting thing is that the blood-sucking vampires got away with it all! I don't believe there was a federal investigation; if there was one, it was very quiet but it should have been publicly broadcast and led to many arrests among the transit system management. Surprisingly, this was not considered enough of a story to ensure world news coverage. I strongly believe this was criminal activity, and those responsible should be held accountable. They should be fired, be demoted, have pay decreases, pay hefty fines, or be imprisoned. If you or I had been in this situation, we would have been shot at, stomped on, spat on, stoned, and protested. We'd have had our hands chopped off, been cursed to hell, and had voodoo dolls made of us. More than likely, a judge would not even give us a trial but would say, "The news coverage was your trial. You should have spoken while you were handcuffed, escorted by the police, and the cameras were in your face. Shut up! Enough! You are guilty! Bury them alive fifty-thousand miles under the earth, and toss the key into a volcano." Now, that would have made the news all over the world.

During my training with the transit system, I was given an abundance of handouts and repeatedly told not only how great the benefits were but most of all that this was a company for families, that we'd feel like our own families were here with us. Management promised to assist us with anything we'd need. If there was a problem, we should feel free to talk to them. They had our backs, and we'd all stick together. Oh, yeah? Well if that is the case, the transit system that I work for is a family of pimps and my name is Yummy the prostitute. No matter how much employees complain, and despite the countless reports we file, nothing changes. Instead, we feel bruised, battered, beat up, bombarded, and bum-rushed. We might be overworked, frustrated, weak, stressed, or sick, but the transit system vehicles must remain in service and fulfill the company motto: get that money. The majority of the responses from headquarters (HQ) are the same. All of these examples are from my real-life personal experiences except for number three, which happened to a coworker. They are listed from least to most important, based on the responses from HQ.

Low Priority

1) I was late and called HQ. "I am forty-five minutes behind my scheduled time. Can you please put me on schedule [i.e., send me out of service until I arrive at the scheduled time point to begin my trip]"? HQ's response: "Run it out [stay in service], or send a text message to run it out."

2) Broken air conditioner. I called HQ. "Please hear me out. It is 105 degrees, which means it is sunny and blistering hot. With the

AC broken, it feels like we are being cooked alive inside an oven. The passengers are pissed off, complaining it is hard to breathe, and they feel like they are suffocating. Could you please give me another vehicle before I get to the end of the line?"

HQ's response: "Operator, you must do a full trip, as is written in your rulebook, before exchanging or swapping vehicles. If the passengers have a problem, give them the option of staying on or getting off and waiting for the next bus. Run it out, operator, and have a good day."

My response: "No, I will not do a complete trip. Once I arrive at the end of the line, I am going out of service. I cannot function, and it is not fair to the passengers. Can you have a supervisor wait for me at the end of the line?"

HQ's response: "Excuse me, operator? Are you telling me that you are not going to follow the rulebook or a direct order"?

My response: "Exactly. I'm using common sense."

I hung up the phone and refused to answer when she called back. I then walked inside of a store to keep cool. My supervisor arrived about two to three minutes later. He entered my vehicle and said, "Hell, no! This vehicle can't go back on the streets. I would be a total jackass to keep you in service." The HQ manager contacted the supervisor, and I could hear the coldness in her voice and feel the spit coming through the phone. The supervisor finally said, "Yeah she's right here with me, and, no, I am not sending her back to the streets in that vehicle. I'd be committing murder." He hung up the phone, shook his head, and thought—I read his mind—*big, ole dummy!* A different vehicle finally pulled up, and back in service I went with nice cold air.

3) A dying person. The operator called HQ. "I have several passengers on my bus. However, there is one passenger in particular who is unresponsive, has urinated on himself, and is drooling heavily.

HQ's response. "Operator, continue in service. A supervisor will meet you along the way to help. I do not want to delay service."

Two supervisors showed up. The first supervisor checked in with the driver but never boarded the vehicle to check on the dying man. The second supervisor did board the vehicle, checked on the unresponsive man, determined he was breathing, and told the operator to continue in service, run it out to the end of the line, and have the police deal with the dying man. When the police boarded the vehicle, they said the man was dead.

The transit system management offered some defensive explanations to the public: If the operator had requested an ambulance or the police, we would have dispatched them immediately. There was no sense of distress or urgency from either the operator or passengers ... therefore all proper protocols were followed. It is quite usual for the transit system operators to carry passengers who are intoxicated or on drugs, especially on the weekends after clubs and bars have closed. An estimated ten people die annually on the transit system vehicles.

The one thing I personally want to express to the operator is, “It is not your fault that the man died. You did not one thing wrong. You were the professional in that situation. You have done everything right. The mass transit system authority is to blame. The death is on our employer’s hands, not yours.” The president of the Transit Workers Union (TWU) could not have said it any clearer. “Once she [the operator] stated … that the individual [was] unresponsive, they would have been brain dead not to consider that to be a possible medical emergency.”

Medium Priority

4) Human waste. The operator called HQ. “A passenger just pulled down his pants and pooped in the front aisle near the front doorway as he was exiting the vehicle. I need to bring this vehicle in now.”

HQ: “Operator, how many trips do you have left?”

Operator: “I’m done once I get to the end of the line.”

HQ: “Okay, I need to know where exactly is the poop? Is it in the pathway of the passengers or along the sides?”

Operator: “What? Are you serious? Why is that important? Have you heard what I just told you?”

HQ: “Operator, I heard you loud and clear. I’m only asking because you are finished once you complete this trip, and I wanted to know if you could still continue in service and have the passengers avoid the waste by stepping over it.”

Operator: “That’s ridiculous! No! Absolutely not!”

HQ: “Aah. Operator, stay put, and I’ll call you back.” A few minutes pass by, and then the phone beeps.

HQ: “Okay, operator, bring the bus in.”

Did you notice that in this scenario HQ did not use the oh-so-famous slogan, “run it out”? But what could possibly compete with human waste in a vehicle?

High Priority

5) The fare box. The operator called HQ. “The fare box is broken, and it is not accepting any money.”

HQ: “Allow the passengers to get on, and do not accept any transfers or take any fares. Make an announcement that Flag Street will be your last stop. I see that you are due at Flag Street at two o’clock. Wait for the Z bus, number 3714. It should arrive at the stand at 2:23 p.m. Call HQ once the exchange has been made."

Simple, short, and sweet, the key phrase is, "not accepting money." It will get you out of damn near any situation. It works nearly every time, without any back-and-forth arguments between the operator and HQ. Notice that I did not have to say one word, and management did not ask any dumb or frustrating questions, such as, "Have you tried kicking and banging on the fare box to see if the money will go down?" The manager's temperament is chill, nice and calm.

The only uncomfortable part of this situation is the reaction of those passengers who are riding farther than Flag Street. Many of them do not want to get off and wait for another bus even if the fare box is broken. And when I tell the passengers who are waiting at the transit stops that Flag Street will be my last stop, once again, those who are traveling farther become aggravated. You can feel the fire coming out of their mouths, smell the smoke coming out of their ears, and see their veins popping in their eyes. The volcano explodes, and every creature on land is on a violent rampage. The gorilla suits are on, and people begin to talk at you: "I hate these damn drivers." "Y'all always do this shit." "This ain't right. Hell, I rode three vehicles without AC today, and now you're putting us off the vehicle because of a broken fare box? Y'all need your asses kicked, bitch." Some people become so overwhelmed they come crying to me with their problems. Others ask if I can call and speak to their employers or daycare centers, or write a note explaining the situation. And of course there are the fools who do not know how to control their actions and become buck wild. These idiots shatter the windows, kick the doors, throw bottles, and break the rear door's mirror. One thing is for sure: an operator with a broken fare box will hardly ever be told to complete a full trip before exchanging the vehicle. The only time you may hear "run it out" is if, and this is a huge if, an operator tells HQ that she is on her last trip, i.e., is driving from point A to point B, her shift is over, and she is returning the vehicle to the depot.

These five, very different, real-life situations are mind-boggling because they are sticky, disgusting, and creepy. If a person falls out of his chair, trembling and shaking on the floor, having a seizure, or a woman screams for the mercy of dear God because she is about to have a baby, transit system managers will say, "Do not delay service. A supervisor will meet you at the next stop to determine if it is a real emergency and whether or not you can continue. How cruel can they be? What makes management's observations so much better than those of the operators who are actually with the passengers? Is management indicating that the operators are unable to determine an actual emergency? And how in the hell does a broken fare box have priority over a broken air conditioner, driving an unconscious person around, and having shit on a bus? The transit system management is heartless and has zero compassion for the staff or the passengers. This is what you call a tragedy. It puts me in the mind frame of slavery. Slave masters stay in the big house, giving orders, keeping all the money that has been made by the hard-working slaves—raping, auctioning, whipping, demeaning, and lynching. And eating well. Meanwhile, the slaves live outside in huts like dogs, work hard on the plantation all year round, making the slave masters rich. They are stripped of their pride and of any joy, have shattered hopes and dreams, receive no respect, and are treated worse than animals, like thrown-away sloppy leftovers or garbage. Morning comes, and it is back to work, without ever hearing a thank you.

Not only are the managers guilty of the mistreating of their employees and mishandling our pension money, but corporations throughout the globe are also traveling to hell on Satan's wing and are being exposed. But that is not enough! Put the faces with the names. The TV news media should expose the corporate criminals to the world as it does local criminals and terrorist leaders and commit them to life in prison. Corruption continues to grow because of money. Money equals power. Everyone wants to be rich and seems to believe that engaging in criminal activity is the only way to accumulate large quantities of money and gain power. Some people wonder about managers' frames of mind and what kind of people they are. Instead of working together, employees and management become divided, and relationships grow sour. We are at odds, and the respect between the two is gone. Many employees feel that there is no way out of this mad situation and simply put up with management's deceiving behavior. These people become like genies in a bottle: your every wish is my command. I strongly believe that management has escaped being investigated by buying people off with hush money to keep them quiet and convince them to overlook fraudulency, theft, and major problems—all to keep from spending time behind prison bars. They also have their press relations officers cover up lies and scandals.

Why have transit system operators suffered these malicious acts of abuse without protection for so many years? For example, one day I arrived at the end of the transit line. A male passenger, approximately six-feet tall and with a thin build waited until all of the passengers had exited the bus and then verbally assaulted and threatened me. He put his hands in my face, called me all kinds of filthy names—"nasty, stinking dirty cunt, you're just a fuckin' bitch"—and shouted terrifying threats such as, "I should whip your ass up and down this vehicle for making me miss my bus. And guess what, there's no one here to help you out. And if the police arrive, I'll already have my satisfaction because I did what I wanted to do to you." Horrified and shaken up, I knew that I was about to get the life beaten out of me. I remained in my upright sitting position and with my left hand frantically pushed the buttons, all of them but the right one, the "help, call police" button. Then something clicked inside of my head, and I said to myself, *C. C., calmly explain your position and hopefully he will understand.*

I said, "Sir, please try and understand my situation. If I arrive at a scheduled time point ten minutes early, a supervisor could be waiting there or I could receive a call from headquarters. There could be a spotter riding my vehicle, watching and recording my every move, who then would report to my managers, and believe me there will be serious consequences." There was a ten-second silence, and he gave me a half smile. Without taking my eyes away from him, I relaxed a little and gave myself an invisible pat on the back. Then this deranged idiot yelled, "You fuckin' liar! Liar! Liar! Liar! Liar! That's bullshit! I take this bus route every day with many different drivers, and every single one of them gets here ten to twenty minutes early every day except for you! None of the drivers ever gets in trouble, and there is never a supervisor waiting here. You can't imagine how pissed off you've made me right now. Let me get off this vehicle before I do more than hurt you."

Once he stepped off my vehicle, I closed my doors, began shaking and crying uncontrollably, and pushed the button to call HQ to ask for the police immediately. The township where I was dispatched the police right away. Within two minutes the police arrived, filling half of the parking lot. He was arrested, spent the weekend in jail, and had a $400 fine. We went to court, and not surprisingly I won my case, with the confusing help of the defendant. The defendant explained to the judge that everything I said about his actions was truthful. His only complaint was that I was lying about facing serious consequences, which made him angry. The judge lowered his head onto his right shoulder and looked at the defendant in confusion; then he asked, "Sir, do you realize what you'd just said?" The defendant replied, "Yes I do." The judge asked, "Are you on any type of medication?" That question tickled the funny bone of everyone in the courtroom. The defendant appealed, but I guess his argument was not worthy of a second hearing and got thrown out.

A coworker's situation made the local news. The operator was driving on the expressway, and a passenger walked up and began punching the operator's face! How insane is that! I believe that lunatic was on a demonic mission to commit suicide and take others down with him. Seeing what that passenger did brought back sad memories of 9/11. My coworker could easily have snapped like a twig and lost control. The vehicle could have spun, turned over, and flipping over, killing other passengers, other motorists, and delaying traffic for hours. If that had happened, you would have thought an earthquake had hit this city. Could you imagine how many police officers, ambulances, helicopters, reporters, cleanup crews, etc., would have been on the scene? How many families would have to be contacted and told that their loved ones had been killed as well as the reason for the massive vehicular accident? I thank the Lord that was not the case. But if a disaster of that type had happened, would the operators have obtained the benefit of having safety features on their vehicles? It sounds like a cruel and horrible thing to say, but this is my reality. Transit system operators have taken a journey through the entire chain of command, pleading for help, from our depot's union representatives all the way to the president of the union. All of the transit system managers and the CEO know our concerns, our dissatisfactions, and about the abuse we receive. There is a Q&A section in one of the local newspapers, specifically directed at the transit system CEO, but he only offers a bunch of hogwash talk when it comes to protecting and investing in the safety of the operators. Management is more focused in raising the fare (every other year) and spending big money on safety features and glamorizing the rail lines (especially in the business district) rather than the bus lines (used by local residents).

However I must admit that cameras have been installed on some of the buses, the only worthwhile safety feature provided by the transit system authority. Operators were told the cameras record images both inside and outside the vehicles and are able to see every detail on every individual person. It is just like watching HDTV. This was to be a step toward making operators safer, but it was hardly enough. Now I have learned that a lot of vehicles are without cameras, and most shocking of all is the revelation that in the buses that do have them, some of the cameras are nonfunctional!

One clear, bright, busy day, I had a bus with a camera. The traffic light had just turned red, and I pulled over into the far right lane to allow passengers to exit and board. I then turned on my left signal and positioned my vehicle in the left lane, ready to pull off. Once the traffic light turned green and I was in the process of pulling off, a minivan that was in the far-left lane decided to play Russian roulette with his and his passengers' lives. He made a right turn in front of my vehicle, but it was too short of a turn, and he struck my vehicle. The van had a huge dent above its right rear tire. The good thing was that only one passenger claimed injury. I had bystanders as witnesses, and the left front bumper of my vehicle was scratched. The damaged van pulled over about fifty feet from me. I called HQ and asked them to send a supervisor, ambulance, and the police, and I walked over toward the van to see if those inside were okay. The man jumped out of his van, gave it a quick look over, flew back into his van, and sped down the street.

Clearly I was a victim of a hit-and-run. The only information I had was the color of the van, the number of people in it, and a description of the driver. I said to my supervisor, "That fool sped off and turned at the next corner on two wheels. You would have thought he was being chased by the cops! The funny thing is, he probably actually believed he'd gotten away with it. Little does he know the camera caught everything, every detail of the accident, and even the description of his van and license plate." We chuckled and after the supervisor finished writing his report, he looked over at me and said, "No, little do you know, the joke may be on you." I gazed at him with a frown on my face. "What do you mean the joke may be on me?" He explained, "The majority of these cameras do not function. There could be one hundred vehicles with cameras on the street. But less than half of them work, and that's with all depots combined." Hearing this completely knocked me off balance. I was about to tell him that I could not go on, that I was sick and needed to go home. With disappointment, I buried my face in my hands and welcomed bitter thoughts into my head: *No, the hell, he did not just tell me this shit! He don't know me! Oh someone in management must have ate him up something nasty! That's ridiculous! That makes no sense! He's lying! How in God's name does he know that? Why, why, why are they giving us false hopes? Why do this to us?*

Why would the transit system invest hundreds of thousands of dollars on plastic-wrapped, brand-spanking, new cameras for the vehicles and not have them work? Why? I took a deep breath, looked at him, and said in a hopeful tone, "I'm waiting for you to say, 'Ah ha! Got you'"! He laughed and replied, "I'm being honest with you. Besides me, there is one other person who travels throughout the depots and actually loads and pulls the disks from all of the vehicles. It costs enormous amounts of money to keep a disk in each vehicle, and it drains the vehicle's battery fast." When I had a moment to sit and digest our conversation, my body began twisting and turning, and going through different changes. At one point, I felt low. My whole demeanor grew sour by the second. My voice was so angry, so deep and rough, it would have turned a mountain into a bump in the road. I was scratching my head, drenched in sweat, with my eyes shut. I was breathing so damn hard, my chest was going in convulsions. The heel of my right foot seemed to be nailed to the floor as I rapidly tapped my toes. My temples were pounding like beating drums, and I had a funky attitude that would make a lion put his tail in between his legs and haul ass the other way. You would have thought my body was possessed by the devil and that I was going through an exorcism. A few seconds later I was high, amped! My body was pumped up, like the Incredible Hulk. I paced back and forth in my house, looking out my windows, thinking I could leap out of them and across the backyard and land inside of a six-foot gate housing three vicious pit bulls and beat the blood out of them with my bare hands. This couldn't happen in my dreams.

(To animal activists all over the world: I am an animal lover! I watch all the National Geographic and Animal Planet channels and shows: *Dogs 101*, *Whale Wars*, *Monster Fish*, *Pit Boss*, *Untamed and Uncut*. You name it, I watch it! I have a big heart for animals, and I am very affectionate with them. I hug and kiss my pet, comb her, rub her tummy, and even clean the gunk from her eyes. You say it, I do it! She is pampered with spa-like treatments, fed the best dog food, eats where I eat, sleeps where I sleep, and gets plenty of exercise. Folks, I am damn good to my pet. So, I beg you, please do not drag my name through the mud and accuse me of animal cruelty. Thank you.)

That most of the cameras do not work was very believable and yet caused disbelief, as if someone had cast a wicked spell over me. Employment with the transit system does not guarantee a positive outlook for our future safety or money. It is simply a dead end. I've spent many years on a losing battle. It never would have occurred to the operators to think that any of the cameras were not operating. For God's sake, it was the responsibility of every operator to take one hour of personal time to be trained on this equipment. Millions of dollars were wasted throughout the years. It has been too long, but now is the time for the transit system operators to stand up and let our voices be heard throughout the world, to insist that management invest in the safety of the employees. Time has proven throughout the years that management does not quite understand how to spend the money and protect their staff. Let me become your safety counselor and guide you toward several healthy, good-quality tips to keep your employees from harm. Put the money where the operators can see, touch, and smell it.

1. Modify the vehicles with hard, thick, fiberglass shields that cover the operators' areas, secured with a master lock. Nothing that is dirt cheap or flimsy. Do not insult us and bargain with our lives for peanuts! We want something unbreakable. People need to recognize that the operators' lives are not to be toyed with. This shield will not only protect us from bodily assaults but also prevent people from hovering over us, coughing or sneezing on us, and hollering in our ears. The protective shields will allow us to have elbow room and will stop bodies and bags from falling on our heads.
2. A personal door for the operator would be another great modification. The door could be installed with a security window and open onto side steps located on the left side of the vehicle. It would allow the operator to move freely onto and off of the vehicle without disturbing the passengers—to remove an object from our path, make an adjustment to the outer parts of the vehicle, or speak to a supervisor outside. It also would be very beneficial in emergencies.
3. Hire undercover and uniformed police officers to ride the vehicles to the end of the line. I do not care whether they are transit officers or the city police. Just do it! Somehow, somewhere, some way, negotiate a deal to make it happen. Having a police officer on board will definitely make me feel less tense and more secure. Passengers will think three times before assaulting anyone. The presence of a police officer will

greatly cut down a lot of violence and bring order throughout the transit system.

4. Station police officers at the end of each transit line to check on the condition of the operators. Let the officers walk through the vehicles. This would be especially helpful for checking on passengers who might be asleep (if not dead), lost, or hostile. Much of the time, chaos breaks out at the transit terminals, even though supervisors are on the spot; often, they need just as much help as the operators. If any operators are involved in a distressing situation on the street, at least the police officer on the beat can radio for backup and promptly come to the rescue. Again, just having police officers stationed at these transit stops will put a halt to a lot of the madness aboard our vehicles.
5. Run it out, and spend that money on advertisements. Transit system operators want to be represented and broadcast throughout the media. Have TV commercials and radio stations announce their importance and also the penalties people will receive for threatening an operator's life—the years they will spend in prison and the hefty fines they will pay. Plaster huge signs all over the stations and the outer parts of the vehicles just as they do with ads for car dealerships, TV shows, department stores, and radio stations. Spend that money, and on billboards across the land to warn the public that assaulting an operator is a serious crime . We want to be unmasked in the same neighborhoods that feature the beer, potato chips, Caribbean vacations, and casinos on billboards. Promote transit operators in the front pages of editorials and

all of the daily newspapers, perhaps on the same page with our CEO's Q&A section.

Do I believe that the transit system authority will pay heed to any of these suggestions? Will they actually sacrifice their luxurious lifestyles to protect their employees? Can management show good faith toward their employees and revive the system? I would like management to explain what the operators have done to the transit system to make you treat us like savages and refuse to take the necessary steps to invest in our health, safety, and welfare? Must we be at war with our own employer? Will management run the risk of being telecast and becoming a big news scandal with interviews, reopened and exposed files, investigations, fines, or imprisonment? Or will they have a bring-it-on attitude and look in the darkness for their lord Lucifer to lead them using the same old weapon—hush money. The transit system has gotten away with dirt for years, but that won't last forever. Violent attacks on transit system operators are rapidly increasing, and there seems to be no end to the situation. Operators should not have to come to work knowing that their lives could be shattered or end at any moment. I surely did not sign up for this. If I had known that working for the transit system would be like fighting in Pakistan, I would have enlisted in the US Special Forces. The transit system is in a state of emergency. Since the urgent call for help is lacking in my city, maybe other cities in the United States and countries around the world can join forces to stop the violence against transit system employees. This list is not in any specific order. I've just randomly listed several cities and countries that I have read about. I am asking for help from the cleanest and safest transit systems in the world:

1. Washington, DC
2. Charlotte, NC
3. Sao Paulo, Brazil
4. Tokyo, Japan
5. Moscow, Russia
6. Phoenix, AZ
7. Salt Lake City, UT
8. Copenhagen, Denmark
9. Madrid, Spain
10. London, England
11. New York, NY
12. Berlin, Germany
13. Montreal, Canada
14. Denver, CO
15. Paris, France
16. Hong Kong, China
17. Taipei, Taiwan
18. Beijing, China

I am begging all the suitable transit systems in the United States and around the world to assist my city and others in the same predicament by providing procedures on safety, cleanliness, and reducing crime. It seems as if my city has not a clue about how to proceed. Knowing that the transit system has the operators' backs and is looking out for our well-being will ensure that we keep focused and relieve our anxiety. We can only perform our jobs well if we feel secure and know that our employer is spending its money wisely to make that happen. If you are a retiree or like me are currently working for a transit system, this book is for us and about us. The invisible people now have a voice. The days of kicking dirt under the rug are over. We need to come together, stand as one, and blow the roofs off the buildings and tell the world about our working environment. I know that I am not the only operator with a story to tell. I plan on visiting every city and state that I can to shake the hands of my fellow coworkers and discuss the crisis that is affecting transit systems and find solutions. I want to visit middle schools and high schools to discuss the students' behavior and their consequences of that behavior, and encourage the young people to use their heads to really think before they act. The transit system needs to correct this situation without any excuses. And transit riders need to stop the violence.

WHEN I THINK about trash, I think about used napkins, candy wrappers, and unwanted furniture. When I think about garbage, I see fruit peelings, wasted food, and insects. But when I vision the city dump, the very first thing that crosses my mind is the smell, which is an automatic knockout. My body cringes from the toxin-filled air of rotten fish, dead animals, sewage, maggots, and rats. The fumes shoot up my nostrils, turning my brain into slush, making my eyes itchy and watery; my face swells and develops multiple rashes. Then I gag and vomit from the awful taste I've gulped down. I feel brain damaged, my equilibrium is off balance, and I am sick and ready to die.

I would like to cautiously welcome you aboard the vehicles of my city's Mass Transit Authority System, which are better known as the city dump. From early in the morning to late at night, people stash garbage throughout the vehicles. Before I make the proper adjustments and am 100 percent comfortable in my seat, I am registering at 85 percent. However, once I am fifty feet away from my vehicle, that repulsive smell alone will bring all of my senses to full attention. I know exactly what you are thinking: "Aren't the vehicles supposed to get cleaned every night"? I will answer the question this way. I have written up countless vehicles for various reasons. A couple days will go by, and I'll be on that same bus, which will still have the exact slip I'd written a couple of days earlier. The only time the vehicles seem to get immediate attention is if the fare box is broken (got to get that money!) or if they contain human waste. Otherwise, the operators either request another vehicle or make use of a broom and dustpan. Yes, the transit system hires maintenance staff to clean the vehicles inside and out. However, there are times when they do not do their jobs.

Once I stepped into a vehicle, you would have thought that I had broken into someone's home. I had stepped into the terror zone and was instantly attacked, with pigeons and roaches on the warpath. The roaches fell off the ceilings and ambushed me while the pigeons aggressively flapped their wings, extended their legs, and charged toward me as if to say,

> Ahn ahn sucker, you want our home, you gotta fight for it. My family's been nesting on this vehicle for hours, safe from the dangers of the forty-mile-an-hour winds, rain and snow, and thunder and lightning. If you think we are leaving without a fight, you must be stupid. You will not disrupt our home or feeding grounds. If you want war, bring it!

It was like that scene from the movie *The Birds*, when the birds began ferociously attacking the woman and she was running for her life. My heart was racing so fast and jumping around; I was petrified. I had to run to the depot and tell management to put me in the sick book. That was my very first time experiencing anything like that. Now I am a pro, used to having critters and fowl play on my vehicle, I treat the situation differently, especially when it affects my pockets. Most of the time I will ask for another vehicle, especially if there is an infestation of critters. If birds are the problem, I will just have a male coworker fight them off. But if there is no one around, I take matters into my own hands: I turn my vehicle on from the rear and then open and close the doors to get their attention so they can fly out and I can avoid being pooped on, getting my hair pulled and having my eyeballs scratched out.

It blows my mind when passengers get on board stuffing their faces with pizza, chicken wings, crabs, ribs, and Chinese food and then have the nerve to complain about the smell or trash on the vehicle. Oh really? How do they think the trash gets onto the vehicles? From spaceships flying overhead and beaming down the garbage? No! The guilty ones are the trifling passengers, who do not seem to care at all about society. I recall talking with my mom about how the passengers leave the vehicles in a complete mess. She was so surprised when I said, "Shoot, I wish it was only newspapers and cigarette butts." You see, my mother has not ridden public transportation for about thirty years, so imagine her reaction when I mentioned buses now have air conditioning and there is no smoking. In the 1970s the vehicles had no air conditioning, and passengers were allowed to smoke and open the windows. My mother is one of those gals who enjoys her car as much as the boys.

Some of these dirty passengers are the ones who invite the infestations of mice, roaches, and insects. If my fellow coworkers and I were given the opportunity to grade the public on behavior and cleanliness, I for sure would give them a big, fat F. I remember pulling up to a stop where approximately twenty to thirty people were waiting to board. As soon as the doors opened, I began slobbering like a dog from the smell of barbeque ribs. When I arrived at the end of the line and checked my vehicle, I found that the passenger had left his rib bones, tray, napkins, and bag in a seat and all over the floor. The same thing has happened with chicken bones, crab shells, french fries, bottles, opened drinks, tomatoes, and pickles picked out of sandwiches; you name it, the vehicles have it. How can people eat full-course meals on a crammed vehicle with other passengers standing over them, sneezing, sniffling, and coughing? That is what attracts rodents, birds, and insects. They smell food and love trash. A handful of passengers are like dogs; even as adults they still need someone to clean up behind them. Another good reason not to eat on transit system vehicles is the respect for others. This is mass transit, transportation for the public, not a personal vehicle. The vehicles are not restaurants or picnic tables at a park. Their purpose is to let people have a comfortable ride and get off.

What About Us?

There are two incidents that I would like to share with you.

Usually, I drive anywhere and everywhere. If I must pay for parking, so be it. This was a beautiful spring day, and I did not have to go too far, so I rode mass transit. On my way home, I chose to visit my mother. I was sitting in the second row behind the driver. To the right of me, there was a well-dressed lady in bright spring colors, sitting in the first row. As people were boarding, the driver stopped a young lady carrying her toddler, who was sucking on a messy, dripping water ice (Italian ice), and said, “Miss, please get rid of that water ice. It is dripping everywhere.” The young lady yelled, “I ain’t getting rid of nothing! I just bought that damn water ice!” She stepped onto the vehicle, her child sucking the dripping water ice, talking on the phone, and searching for her fare. The well-dressed lady got everyone’s attention when she stood up and said sternly, “Excuse me, miss. Please do not sit next to me with that water ice in your child’s hand.” Everyone froze and began staring at one another and whispering. You would have thought everybody on the vehicle was at a church gathering, except that what we were saying was, “Aw, shit. Please do not sit next to that lady. Please don’t.”

But she and her messy child sat down next to the well-dressed lady. And if that were not bad enough, she also talked about the bus driver and the lady to the person on her phone. Fast forward! Guess what? The child dropped the water ice all over the lady’s outfit. The lady jumped up and hollered, “Bitch! I warned you not to sit your ass next to me!” The power in her voice made the child jump out of his mother's lap. The lady's knuckles landed on the young mother's eye, and she fell hard into the middle of the aisle. One passenger grabbed the crying child away from the action while the rest of the passengers and I quickly moved out of the way. However, the well-dressed lady was not done. She finished the young mother off with a few more punches to the face. As the young mother lay there, damn near motionless with a swollen face, the furious lady stood over and said, "Your ass whipping is the reason why you should not bring food on the bus." She then pulled the bell and got off at the next stop. A male passenger helped the battered young mother up and sat her next to the lady holding her crying child. She sat with her back toward the passengers, in shame, comforting her child.

In this second incident, I was the operator of the bus rather than a witness. As I was pulling up to a stop, I saw a man running out of a doughnut and coffee shop with a hot beverage in his hand. When he walked past me, the aroma from the coffee had me on cloud nine. Now, just about everyone knows that this shop's hot beverages are piping hot. You can purchase a medium-hot hazelnut coffee, add three creamers, two packets of sugar, and one packet of sweetener at 7 a.m., wait an hour to take a sip, and that coffee will still be hot.

In addition, this baby mama wanted to board the crowded vehicle with an open baby stroller the size of a punch buggy (Volkswagen Beetle). Before she stepped on I told her, "Miss, as you can see, my vehicle is packed. So for the safety of your child, could you please remove your baby from the stroller and fold it? Giving me attitude and a few choice words, the baby mama got on, with the baby in the stroller, through my back doors, assisted by other passengers. Shortly after I drove off, an idiot ran directly in front of my vehicle, which caused me to slam on my brakes. This sort of thing happens all of the time, just about every single day. That is when I heard the scream of death. The passengers in the rear shouted at me to stop the vehicle. I heard a whole lot of swearing and loud crying, which shook me up. I carefully pulled the bus over to the side to allow other vehicles to pass by safely, put my parking brake on, and opened both doors. In a trembling voice, I asked the passengers nearest to me, "What happened?" They had no clue and were trying to find out the details.

The woman with the stroller was screaming and yelling out, "My baby! Oh, my God, please help my baby!" My supervisor and a police car just happened to be driving toward my vehicle. They pulled over and stopped in front of me. The supervisor and one of the police officers walked through the crowd of passengers, who said, "The bus driver told the girl to fold her stroller before getting on but she wouldn't listen." The officials approached me and asked what had happened. I told them the truth, "I do not know. I have no knowledge of the incident." I found out a few minutes later from the other police officer that when I slammed on my brakes, the hot beverage was knocked out of the man's hand and into the stroller of the four-month-old baby. Thank goodness, the baby was not critically injured, but his mother was completely rattled.

I asked my supervisor for the mandatory information, including his car number to identify who was at the scene, for my accident report. He replied, "Not a problem. First, let's see what the cops need from you." But the officers said, "No, she's clear. She didn't witness the incident." My supervisor asked, "Did you contact headquarters or hand out any incident cards [for collecting names, addresses, phone numbers, and comments of the witnesses]?" I nervously but without hesitation said, "No." He responded, "Don't beat yourself up over it. You were not a witness, and the police did not need your information, so there is no need for you to write up an incident report. I'll handle it." I did exactly what he said, and he put me back on my scheduled time (i.e., I went out of service, drove to my scheduled time point, and then went back into service). A couple of years have passed, and I have never heard one word about that incident from a union rep or management.

Sadly, both these terrible incidents involved women and their children. Transit system operators have the passengers' best interests in mind when we ask them to stop or start doing something. These two unfortunate incidents could have been prevented if those passengers had only listened to the operators.

Often these incidents lead to waste issues that affect mass transit vehicles. Shoes stick to the floors because of spilled drinks, gum, and candy. Bottles and cans roll back and forth between people's feet. Women and girls pick or comb their hair weaves and braids as if they were in a salon and toss the hair pieces in the seats and on the floors. Empty junk food bags, chips, and newspapers are left in seats or scattered on the floor. One of the worst things is sunflower seeds. They resemble an army of bugs and are difficult to sweep up. Finally, I know I've mentioned this quite a few times throughout this book, but who in their wildest nightmare would expect human waste to be a major problem aboard mass transit vehicles. Well, it is. And yes, many of the aisles and seats that riders walk on and occupy have been soiled with human urine and poop. Throughout my years as a transit system operator, I can line up every route that I've had, beginning with my very first human-waste incident. Take a deep breath, hold your nose, and cover your mouth because it is a stinker.

I picked up a medium-built grown man who appeared to be in his late thirties to mid-forties. He seemed to be worn out and just wanting to go home. He sat in the outer seat in the first row of seats behind the operator. Sitting in a slightly slouched position, his legs were wide open, and his left arm was straddled on the seat next to him as he was looking out of the window. About two minutes after this man got on, he passed gas so loudly it sounded like a ship's horn. I covered my nose and mouth and looked at him in the rearview mirror in disbelief. A woman yelled out, "Oh, my God! Please tell me he did not just shit on himself!" She was livid. As I pulled over into the transit stop, the other passengers got up from their seats and walked to the rear of the vehicle, cussing at the man. I immediately called headquarters and opened the doors to allow the passengers, myself, and that hazardous smell to get off. The vehicle smelled like a barnyard. Everyone exited the vehicle, except for the man, who sat in all his filth with his arms folded and a creepy smirk on his face.

I entered my vehicle and, before answering my beeping phone, stated, "Sir, my vehicle is out of service, and you have to get off." As I began explaining the incident to headquarters, the man stood up, held on to his right pants leg and began to wiggle, shake, and kick his leg like he was kicking a biting mutt away from his ankles. Ten pounds of flying mashed poop went everywhere. I stood in my seat with my sweater covering my face and my back pushing against the side window, begging headquarters to send help. I was not going to chance running off of the vehicle and having poop and pee splatter on me. Then the man walked off the bus, leaving a trail of pee and poop juice behind him. By the time my supervisor came, the man was out of sight. Although I had one more trip to do, I returned the vehicle to the depot. Another operator completed the trip, and I went home.

This next story is just as puke-causing. As nasty as these stories are, they are also true. I need to tell members of the public what they are stepping into when they ride on mass transit vehicles. If your lip gloss falls onto the floor or seat, you had better think three times before using it on your lips. Or if you dropped your pen or pencil on the seat, think before placing it into your mouth or you may have a freaky fungus growing on your face, which reminds me of my next story.

The regular transit operator was on vacation, and I was to replace him until his return. I had three weeks to complete this route before I moved on to the next one. The behavior of the passengers toward a new driver always amazes me. That is not to say that they are not uncontrollable with the regular operator—at times, they are—but when they become familiar with an operator, they develop an unexplainable respect for you. In my case, these passengers had no respect for the rookie.

I was either the last or the next-to-last vehicle to pull in for the evening. It was a Friday after midnight (something about Friday nights makes people lose their minds), pitch black outside with limited street light, and I was the only person occupying the vehicle. Along this strip, there was a wide range of fast-food restaurants, shopping areas, and prisons. At every stop, I picked up male restaurant employees. Late nights on this route I did not see any sign of a woman until I reached the mall, which was approximately forty minutes away. That point was where I met my comfort zone. Before I reached the mall, some of these grown men acted as if they had no home training. My vehicle became the party vehicle. The only thing missing was loud music. Some men got on and fell asleep, but the others were loudly talking, gambling, smoking, eating, drinking. Of course, they trashed the vehicle. Monday through Thursday their behavior was less rowdy. I guess they waited until Fridays to smoke and gamble.

One Friday, I finally spoke up. “Can you please quiet it down,” I said, “because I cannot concentrate.” One of the men approached me and said, “Aw, you hungry? You need a drink?” I ignored him, and he returned to the back of the vehicle, saying in a joking manner, “Yo, she’s mad, and she’s about to call the cops. Y’all better shut the fuck up.” Among all the words that were said in response I clearly heard one guy say, in a stiff voice, “She don’t want to do that, especially when I’m losing.” The others agreed. I wanted to cry, disappear, and call for help, but I was too nervous and afraid. I thought, *What have I just done?* These men had not thought about me until I had opened my mouth. Then I heard two hard hits coming from the back. In alarm, I looked in my rearview mirror and saw mystified expressions on the men’s faces as they also turned to face the rear. I saw two men standing in the seats, urinating out of the window. Some of the passengers made critical remarks toward these losers; the others and I were in complete shock. Then this man sitting near the front said in a loud baritone voice, “Yo, I don’t believe y’all just did that.” One of the morons said, “Man, it was either the steps or out the window.” The baritone man replied, “Yo, I’m tired and right now she’s my only ticket home. How about leaving her alone? Yo, Paul, let me holler at you.” Then the man with the baritone voice turned to me and said, “Miss, don’t bother the cops. You don’t got to worry about them.” I did not think the man was aware of his surroundings, because he seemed to be asleep. The faces of the others expressed rage, and yet they all listened to him as if he were their father and said nothing to him.

I thought, *What just happened? You know what? I don’t even care. Thank you, thank you, and thank you, whoever you are.* The following week, when the men entered the vehicle, the vast majority did not part their mouths to even say hello, which was A-okay with me. I loved it. However, their behavior remained the same with three exceptions: 1) the volume was turned down, 2) there was no smoking, and 3) there was no peeing out of the windows. They could not resist leaving me with one thing, however, and made sure they brought it to my attention. “Watch your step back there,” one of them said. They were not lying. The back of my vehicle was a city dump. The food from the restaurants where these pigs worked was thrown everywhere. They did not miss a spot. These scavengers also used the back door as their bathroom. Abominable is an understatement for that scene. Have you ever been in a position where you do not know what to think or how to feel, when you are entirely comatose? Well, that was exactly how I felt after that frightening episode. After driving to the depot, I checked off “human waste” and wrote that it was all over the back door steps.

Because I was fresh out of training with the mass transit system authority, you might have thought I contacted headquarters and had this incident written up. I did not. I honestly did not know that the beastly behavior of these sorry men would be classified as an incident. As outrageous and appalling as their behavior was, I was too embarrassed to actually have my supervisors and the police officers come to my bus and view this disgraceful scene. During training, my instructor gave many different examples of major and minor accidents and incidents, but nothing in the range of something so horribly vile. To me, that was off the radar. So, of course, I choked because I only had a few weeks on the job.

I knew that I could speak with a union rep about work issues, but I did not know to what extent or, furthermore, what the union's main purpose was. This was my first job with union representation, so I did not have any confidence in my union's support for me. I was overwhelmed by the contract talks over pay roll, wages, prescription plans, etc., and thought what the union was pursuing on the employees' behalf was too good to be true. I was proven wrong. I believed I'd made the best decision simply because I was the only woman in the situation, surrounded by a bunch of low-life men without protection. I believed that if I had written an incident report, my employer would notify those restaurants and send me back onto that same exact route to face those same exact men. Hell, no! Not me! No way was I about to throw myself under the bus. It did not hit me that I had been involved in a major incident until I spoke with my union representative, who said I had several options. He understood why I held back and advised me to try not to allow myself to be subjected to offensive behavior aboard my vehicle. I could have called headquarters and stated that I was not safe and was driving under dangerous conditions. Headquarters would have contacted the police, and the police would have removed the men or explained the consequences if they continued their behavior on my vehicle. I could have written up an incident report expressing my fears and concerns for my safety and that I did not want to work on that particular route or did not want those men on my vehicle. I would have been placed on another route. More than likely, the restaurants along that strip and the police would have been contacted. The police and a supervisor would have checked in on me throughout the evening.

So, yes, I had several options, but I allowed my fears to destroy my confidence.

Since then, I've gotten to know my union representatives and have seen them personally fight and bargain with my employer regarding my position. I have familiarized myself with some of the contract rules, and discussing those rules with my union reps has increased my trust and confidence in them. I now understand that I had put myself in harm's way. That was one of the most inhuman and memorable incidents of indecent behavior I've ever encountered on a mass transit vehicle. Aboard these vehicles, indecent behavior seems to be the norm nowadays, from almost every generation. It does not matter which direction you turn; from the kids to the grown folk, they are tainted. Their behavior is obnoxious, and they themselves are trifling. They almost always leave the vehicles looking like a pigpen. Some people do not feel comfortable unless they are in the middle of filth. I guess slop makes them relax and feel right at home. Mass transit vehicles are where the ugly and dirty come to act like fools and dump their garbage. Their behavior could be the topic of an episode for the Jerry Springer show, which reminds me of another detestable incident.

There were a lot of passengers sitting in the vehicle. The ride was rather easy and quiet. A woman with a baby entered and sat in the first row of seats. A few minutes later, I snapped my neck and gasped from the odor of chitlins. I looked in my mirror and saw the woman changing her baby's diaper. Everyone remained calm, and there were no rude remarks. She then disposed of the baby's diaper behind the seats. I immediately said, "Excuse me, miss. Can you take what you just threw behind that seat with you when you leave?" She was quite embarrassed; she knew exactly what I was referring to and replied reassuringly, "Oh, I am. I just didn't want to hold it around my baby." I said to myself, *Yeah, right*, but to her I said, "Thanks." To my surprise, she picked up the soiled diaper without any back talk. When the lady got off the vehicle, she walked to my side window and smeared the soiled diaper all over it. The only thing that I could say was, *Thank you, Jesus, that my window is shut.* I drove off with my head hung low, thinking somebody please, just shoot me. Two stops away there was corner store and a gas station. I pulled the vehicle over and announced to my passengers that I had to go to the store and get something to clean my window. I brought three extra-large water bottles and a bottle of liquid soap, mixed the two liquids together, and threw it all on the window. At the end of the line, I was scheduled for lunch. The corned beef special that I could not wait to sink my teeth into had to be thrown away. Not only did she kill my hunger, but she also ruined the rest of my day. Everyone eating a chocolate chip cookie or carrying a bag of fruit reminded me of diarrhea. Some of my favorite aromas—the lovely scents of perfumes, sweet potato pie, roasted coffee, and microwave buttered popcorn—now disagreed with me. The only thing that I could force down my throat was Pepto-Bismol, and I only drank that to get some shuteye.

To degrade themselves aboard mass transit vehicles in this way, some people must be worth less than a piece of scrap. How long will this continue? Something needs to be done about this offensive behavior. Obviously, installing cameras in the vehicles is not enough. These criminals believe that the mass transit vehicles are one huge playground. Their savage behavior is the work of wild animals, and untamed animals belong in cages. Trash cans are located at many transit stops. Is it too much to ask them to hold on to their trash until they are off the vehicles?

It is a damn shame how ignorant folk can mess up a good thing for people who are trying to live right. Many passengers complain and ask, "Why do they (the transit bosses) always put beat-up vehicles in our neighborhoods while people in other areas of the city ride on the newer vehicles?" The answer is that when the vehicles are in your neighborhoods, they are vandalized and trashed by the ignorant folk who do not want to do better, who want a free ride in life, and who hate those who work for their success in life. You will continue to get the old, broken-down vehicles until the people in your neighborhood work together to make your voices heard and persuade the ignorant to change their gross behavior. Why should the transit authority have to post signs for grown-ups and teenagers listing standards for human conduct that their mommas should have taught them? What is the point of plastering "do not eat or drink" posters on the vehicles if the transit system is not enforcing any penalties to prevent the ongoing problem of trash on the vehicles?

THERE ARE MILLIONS in my generation (children of the 1970s and 1980s) who were raised the same as I was—with a belt in one hand and a brick in the other, that is, with an iron fist. I was taught the difference between good and bad, kindness and harshness, yes and no, able or unable, right and wrong, and asking and taking, and also that there are consequences for my actions. If I displayed a bit of a funky attitude, oh, it got handled immediately. For instance, my mother was always looking for something odd to place on her mantel or hang on her walls. Mumbling under my breath would have gotten my esophagus snatched out of my neck. My throat would have become that show piece on the mantel, polished and sparkling like a diamond, and the rest of my body would be framed and pinned on the wall as an exhibit. And when my mother took us out, she did not care how angry we were; if someone spoke or greeted us with a hello or good morning, if we did not want to be the lamb in the lion's den, we had to respond with a smile and a "Hello, good morning, and how do you do? Lovely day today, wouldn't you agree?" Throughout my childhood my parents had zero, zip, none, not a drip of tolerance for a disrespectful child living under their roof.

Now as an adult I still adhere to those same teachings. It is okay to be upset because it is a human emotion. But when someone greets you, it is also human decency to return the same gesture. People are not mind readers, and people do not wear their emotions on their faces. However, I say that mass transit riders are different. Fighting traffic is a given, but dealing with the disgusting attitudes of the public is haunting. On a bright cheerful and sunny day, I could see that dark, misty cloud with lightning and flying rattlesnakes hovering over their heads as I pulled into the transit stops. When the passengers stepped onto my vehicle, I greeted them with a warm smile and a "Good morning." Their facial expressions were priceless. From their body language and reactions, you would have thought I was speaking a foreign language. They began gritting on me as if they wanted to smack me, gave me a full-body look over as if they were picking me out of a criminal lineup, rolled their eyes, and walked away without saying anything. These passengers seemed to be possessed with venomous anger. Eyebrows were flipped upside down. I looked into the mirror, and they gave me the evil eye, their mouths twitching from side to side. I said to myself, *These women cannot be mad every time they see me, because I did not do one thing to them.*

I really did not know how to respond. First I thought maybe I was speaking too loudly; then I thought to myself, *I'm not yelling, so that cannot be the reason for their rude behavior.* So I took my tissue and began wiping any leftover crust that might have been in my eyes and blowing into the palms of my hands to get a whiff of my breath. I'd soaped up, put on deodorant, and brushed my teeth for about three minutes before leaving for work, but the "jump back, damn you scared me" reactions had me retracing my morning three times over. After a few days on the J-O-B, I realized that I was not the cause of these passengers' disgruntled attitudes. Some people are just angry. Sometimes the kinder someone is, the uglier the angrier the other person becomes. There have even been a few times where I have gotten barked at for saying "good morning." If I do get a response, it is a "whatever" or "she gets on my nerves with all that good morning."

What I never expected was a woman to stand in front of me and sourly say, "Yeah, yeah, yeah. With you, it's a good morning every damn day." I replied with a smile on my face, "It sure is, and thank you for noticing. You have yourself a good day." She rolled her eyes and slowly walked away. I believe that there are people who actually wake up angry and do not give themselves a fair chance at life. Before leaving their homes in the morning, they plan a day of how to be a jackass. And guess who the first person on their hit lists is? The transit operator, who is the first person they see between the hours of 4 a.m. and 6 a.m.

What better way is there to start your morning than with a friendly face saying good morning? Am I driving you nuts because I say good morning? Do you dislike me because I say good morning?

Do you dislike me for making eye contact? Do you dislike my smile? Do you dislike the soft but strong tone of my voice? Am I too cheerful? Do you want to hurt me because I say good morning? Will you put me on your "kill list" saying it? How does saying a good morning become such a negative issue? I believe that only a mentally ill person who is living in a condition of disgrace can answer that question, or perhaps a licensed therapist. A lot of people on their way to work bear the same demeanor: overly sensitive, feisty, and fidgety. Even someone saying "excuse me" will set them off. They sit and walk around with a grim facial expression that screams "do not stand next to me, do not say my name, do not ask me for anything, just do not bother me." Here is a suggestion: they should get into a canoe and drift into unknown waters. I guarantee that no one will ever bother them again.

Everyone who looks at them is accused of having eye problems. Their negative thoughts are converted into gossiping bitchy cliques (that do not exclude men) and jealousy, which makes them prejudge some and dislike others. Then, of course, they begin to blame everyone but themselves for their headaches and their stressful, overburdened lives. Most of the time I do not know the difference between their butt holes and their mouths because every word they speak is foul. I believe the toxins within some of these riders have them so absentminded that they are unaware that their bodies and brains are on the verge of self-destruction. I am sure this type of behavior is affecting their promotional opportunities at work and personal lives at home. While I do not have a Ph.D., I have been in the company of many overemotional people and have seen the outcomes firsthand. I am just an ordinary, laidback, easygoing chick who knows how to make the ways of life work in my favor despite having an unsafe, underpaid, and extremely difficult job. Unless passengers are willing to change their behavior, their lives will continue to spiral downhill. Everyone has shortcomings in their lives. How you deal with it and overcome it is the key to developing your personality and shaping your future. Just because someone has had a few trees full of rotten bananas doesn't mean he should allow his frustrations turn into negative thoughts. Rotten fruit happens to the best of us. It may leave your mouth with a sour taste but eventually you will get over that moment and move on to the sweet aromas of the next one. Pick yourself up, brush yourself off, meditate to get your thoughts straight, and form a new plan move on to the next tree or into a different direction. The choice is all yours.

Life is about knowing your weaknesses, having the courage to step out on your own to find your strengths, and owning the will to get yourself balanced and learn from your mistakes. Failures belong to those people who have fallen down and dwell in self-pity. Success belongs to those who failed but refused to be held down and got back up with determination. Failures and successful outcomes are everlasting and natural life occurrences. There is nowhere to run or hide. We all must face the courses of life. Every day life teaches a lesson. It hands out experiences, challenges your faith, aggravates your weaknesses, and tests your strengths. Whether the annoyance has to do with your home, kids, mate, coworkers, waiter, bill collectors, or a mass transit operator, you must learn how to take control of your angry emotions and think about your actions and reactions.

My parents and a host of relatives have taught me that anger is a natural emotion. Anger can poison the mind and body, but releasing it can be healthy. Being angry all of the time can kill you by causing unnecessary stress. Now the question is how to release that anger. There is a problem, for example, when a crime is committed in anger. When I was a youngster, a rebellious child would have to confront her parents. Nowadays, that may be the case with a toddler. But kids in middle and high school will shrug their shoulders and tell you, “So what? Go right ahead.” However, for an unruly adult who commits a crime out of anger, the consequences are either life-threatening injuries, prison, or death. That is too much unnecessary time and energy. Every day I tell myself that I will make tomorrow a better day. Who else can determine my inner happiness better than I? And I always expect the unexpected. My way of thinking keeps my soul strong, my body healthy, my spirit alive, my eyes afloat, and my mind ahead of the game. Whenever I feel dreary, just hearing someone say good morning to me lifts my spirit. Somehow it comforts me and makes me acknowledge that there is some good in this world. What I will not do is randomly bring others into my troubles. Most of my thoughts are concerned with self-scrutiny and challenging myself with questions like the following: how will I make this work? I cannot avoid it, so how can I handle it? How can I make a situation peaceful? How can I remain calm and pleasant?

What About Us?

It is not difficult for me to dig within to find peace and happiness. I know that my joy can never be taken from me due to the good life I live and the God I know. My joy lives in my heart, dances with my soul, and enhances my spirit. As I see it, my faults and mistakes are lessons that I can embrace, forgive myself for, and learn and move on from. I take along with my journeys my upbringing, experiences, and thoughts. I've learned how to control my anger by trading it for several healthy activities. I love to be consoled in complete quietness; that is how I calm my mind and start to breathe easy. To allow the process of complete relaxation float over me, I always light sweet, warm, soothing candles; listen to soft, velvety music ("Cruisin'," "Ebony Eyes," "Just My Imagination"); enjoy a long and hot shower; and top it off with a drink. I have a good relationship with my son and decent friends. I play with my dog, I travel, and I basically have a life of good fortune and wealth outside of my job. I view life as a realistic game that must be played to survive. You must work hard to live the legitimate American dream. If you punk out, your life will be at stake. The underworld will chew you up, spit you out like lava fire, and turn you into stone. To survive you must know that the world owes you nothing. Dwelling in hate and self-pity is not the answer.

However, there is one important question that I would like all these unhappy folk to answer: why are you angry? What is the point of being angry every day? It is impossible that you are accomplishing anything good. Usually angry people need the company of others to help keep the negative energy spinning. Your anger is diluting your opportunity to achieve something great and worthwhile in life.

The only person who suffers is you. I believe many people are in a state of depression and may not know it. From what I have read, depression is a serious medical condition that can be treated with help. How would a loved one trying to help a depressed person go about getting help? Medication would be my last resort. Instead, I would make time to help her share her life with me. I would alleviate some of the stress by giving compliments, getting a few laughs in, or getting some exercise, something simple, like walking and having an easy, fun conversation. We could meet at a café for lunch, catch a movie, go to a museum, or discuss a book we are reading. If I do not see, feel, or believe my friend's condition is improving, then encouraging her to seek medical help would be the next step. If you are a depressed person, I truly pray for the better you and hope that you will allow the needed help to enter into your life. Do not let depression destroy you. And do not allow depression to destroy the person you love and care about.

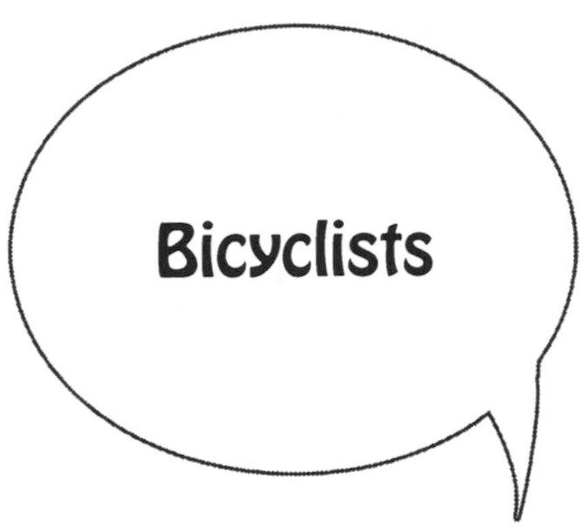

There is a sticker posted inside of mass transit vehicles that states something like, "Watch day and night for bicyclists on your right." If only that were true, I would not have road rage, multiple whiplash incidents, or need to drink a tall glass of Long Island Iced Tea every night before bed. This drink has helped me to fall asleep and get me through the night peacefully without dreaming about how many ways there are to kill a biker. This job will turn you into an alcoholic. I really do understand why so many who work for the transit system have high blood pressure, alcoholism, and drug addiction. It would be nicer, much easier, and safer to travel the streets if bicyclists used the provided bike paths and pulled over when motorists are backed up for five city blocks. But many bicyclists do not do so. They are like ants, scattered everywhere. They cause major problems and are dangerously in the way of motorists. They put a damper on traffic flow and are constantly darting in and out of moving traffic, which causes heated arguments that can lead into violence.

With every bicycle incident, I get a screaming headache. These bicyclists do whatever they want, whenever and wherever they want to do it. On many occasions I have witnessed bicycle accidents in the street and on the sidewalks, everything from minor to damn-near-fatal injuries. Bicyclists swerve in and out of traffic like ping pong balls. They lose their balance and fall, crash into parked and moving vehicles (then take off and ride in a different direction before the motorists open their doors), knock off side mirrors, collide with people and knock them down, run through stop signs and traffic lights, and bike the wrong way down the street. And you know what else? Many times, the bicyclists keep going and are not penalized. So why should they care if they damage someone's vehicle or break the law? Some bicyclists are getting away with crime. There are no license-plate numbers for people to record or photograph. Therefore, they continue to travel recklessly without any repercussions. At times, I wish that I had the ability to disappear into tranquility whenever someone or something crawls under my skin. But when dealing with some of these careless bicyclists, I do not have time for wishing. In my mind, I transform both myself and my vehicle into the demonic car movie character Christine and try to flatten them.

For instance, once when I was on a two-lane street, I had more than enough space to drive around a bicyclist. Other vehicles went around the bicyclist, who was riding too slowly and occupying the entire one side of the lane while eating a hotdog or a doughnut. As I sat at the traffic light, the bicyclist caught up with me and began banging hard along the vehicle, startling me and the passengers, until he reached my window. My window was partially open; he stuck his hand through and tried to grab me, but I slammed it shut with such force that if he had not removed his hand, it would have been chopped off. He yelled, "You fuckin' bitch! Don't you ever go around me again! You don't know who you're messing with! I'll stop these buses from coming into this neighborhood." I said to myself, *Dude, really? I never came close to nipping you.* The passengers standing by my side shouted to the biker, "Asshole! Get the hell out of here! You're not stopping anything!" I gave him a quick look, rolled my eyes, and pulled off. He spat on my window, gave me the finger, and rode away. The passengers were blown away by this. They said this was unreal.

This particular route is considered to be the longest in the city. Transit operators call it the "ghetto line." Every day this line produces loud, ignorant, rude, or crazy people. One day, it was close to noon; traffic was bumper to bumper but moving steadily. I was roughly five to seven minutes behind schedule and twenty minutes away from the end of the line, where I could relax for fifteen minutes. However, during the last twenty minutes of my trip, a bicyclist slowed traffic down to a crawl. There were the bicyclist, two vehicles, and my vehicle. The people in the first car yelled at the bicyclist to pull over, which he did not, and we all began honking our horns. Here is where the senseless games came into play. The bicyclist remained in front of traffic for a couple of blocks, arguing with the driver of the vehicle behind him, which was nearly on top of him. As if I were not doing the turtle walk already, this whole ordeal caused me to stop repeatedly to put enough distance between us so I could drive at a normal pace. The hostile argument led the people in the first car to throw an object at the bicyclist, which caused him to swerve and crash into a parked vehicle. Two guys driving behind the bicyclist jumped out of their vehicle and ran toward the rider, who ran away, leaving his bicycle behind. One of the guys picked up the bike, threw it in the back of his vehicle, and drove off. I called headquarters to inform them about this situation and my whereabouts and to ask them if they could put me back on schedule, which surprisingly they did. Otherwise, I would have been thirty to forty minutes behind my scheduled time.

If a twenty-five-ton trash truck that stops at home after home and block after block can pull over at an intersection or drive around the corner to prevent traffic buildup, why can't a noodle-weight bicyclist give the same respect? There are a few roads that should be banned from bicyclists due to the many dangers. These roads are not expressways; however, they do require accelerated speeds. Open roads with bike lanes allow motorists and bicyclists to wind in and out of traffic. I have observed motorists causing bicyclists using the bike lane to lose control and fall or swerve into the path of oncoming traffic. Multiple times I have seen bicyclists crashing into the rear of a car. This next incident occurred on a compact, four-lane, twisting, semi-expressway. It has a scenic view with rocky hills, trees, and a body of water that stretches alongside. The road has such dangerous curves that at certain points motorists are unable to see around them. One afternoon, I was driving on this road in my personal vehicle, and this shiny, black car with tinted windows zoomed past me. After driving around a few curves and past the police station, I saw a man in a black suit standing in the road next to the shiny, black car waving his badge at two bicyclists, who were standing next to him. I was the first vehicle in the outer lane to approach him and stopped; the other vehicles following did so too. The man asked if I and the driver of the vehicle next to me could turn our blinkers on and follow the bicyclists to where he could pull them over safely. We complied, and he thanked us. That drive was less than five minutes. It was a blessing from God that the man reached those bicyclists before I or the other motorists did, because that surely would have been a mass destruction. There is a safe biker's path that travels the distance of the river, however the road is considered one of America's deadliest. Why the bicyclists were on the dangerous road instead of the biker's path, I do not know. So yes, bicyclists absolutely should be forbidden from sharing this road and others like it with motorists.

Clearly, not every road is meant for bicyclists. I have had bicyclists hold on to my vehicle or attach some kind of rope onto the rear bumper of the bus so they could be dragged down the street. Mass transit vehicles are known to make sudden and unpredictable stops. You had better back up off my tail if you do not want to become part of my tire tread. There also is about one to three feet of space between my vehicle and a parked car and moving vehicles on either side of me. Why in the world would bicyclists sandwich themselves in a space that is no wider than a three-year-old, turning that three feet of space into three inches of space. Do they not care about the predicament they are in? Do they realize the position they put mass transit operators in, how at any given moment a bus driver could give them the blow of death and squash them like a grape? This is not a game! They are throwing themselves in the way of these forty-ton vehicles that will kill them. If they want to play, they should go to the arcade and knock themselves out. They can drive, fly, and fight all they want to with joysticks and handle bars. However, if they want to commit suicide, they should do me a favor and do it on their own damn time and not pull anybody into their death wish. These reckless bicyclists will turn me from Dr. Jekyll into Mr. Hyde in a wink of an eye. They are like a mosquito bite on the sole of my foot—annoying!

There are reasons bike paths exist:

1. to keep bicycles and their riders safe and out of the motorist lane
2. to organize and maintain the flow of traffic
3. to keep bikes off the sidewalks

All three reasons are to ensure the safety of the travelers on the roads.

Since bicyclists use the street, why not enforce the traffic laws? Require bicyclists to take classes educating them about the law, commuting, and safety. Introduce more laws, if necessary, e.g., make bicyclists travel with a certificate, sticker, and an ID to prove their bikes are registered if they are ever pulled over. Wearing protective gear is a must—helmets, knee pads, elbow pads, and, during twilight hours, fluorescent gear. I have seen plenty of bloody mouths and limbs on fallen bicyclists. Bicyclists should be required to have mirrors, reflectors, and license plates, and they should travel in designated bike lanes. They should stop at stop signs and red lights rather than glide through them. They should not wear headphones or ride against opposing traffic. Fine them whenever they break the law.

When will the time be right for the city's councilmen and councilwomen to enforce the bicycle laws? There needs to be collaboration among the council members, bicycle coalition (a nonprofit organization whose mission is to make bicycling safe and enjoyable), bicycle advocates, businesses and their employees, the public, and the media to discuss the importance of bicycle laws, safe bicycling, and stiff fines. The number of bicyclists is multiplying, so why not include them in daily news reporting? Perhaps there could be a segment updating bicyclists on road conditions due to heavy traffic, weather, and men-at-work areas? Bicyclists could express their concerns about their daily commutes, improvements the city needs to make, and their safety tips. What better way is there than to get bicyclists involved with implementing and improving safety and road conditions? And if that is not the answer, what must people do to be heard? Motorists, bystanders, and bicyclists are being victims of reckless bicyclists, a huge problem that is being taken lightly. There are profound offenses that need to be addressed. Though I have neither witnessed nor heard about any fatalities, I am quite sure there have been a few. I believe there would be fewer offenses if only the bicycle laws were enforced. I totally understand the whole concept of going green to save the planet. Living long and maintaining a healthy lifestyle is definitely part of my plan. The thought of less smoke polluting the air and smoke-free facilities is appealing. And bicycling is a great source of exercising. However, the big city I reside in is not a bicycle-friendly, happy-go-lucky city. I live in a big city where both the boys and the girls like their toys. Styling and profiling in their wheels is the name of the game. People want what they want when they want it. They want to get where they are going quick, fast, and in a hurry. They do not want to be sweaty or half-dead, look starved, feeling like they just got the life sucked out of them. Hell no. When it is hot, they want to be able to flick on that AC and when it is cold, the heat.

These drivers do not have the time to throw water all over themselves to cool off and keep from dehydrating. If they want to ride a bike, they will take a camping trip or enroll at a gym. Enough beating around the bush: the car rules, period. It is the main source of transportation. Nonetheless, I believe we can get along and share the road with bikes if we use some creative thinking. There could be a policy put in place to design a friendlier atmosphere between motorists and bicyclists.

Classes on road etiquette should be taught not only to bicyclists but also to motorists. Add bicycle education to the classes taken by those trying to obtain a driver's license or find employment as a driver. Create bigger and color-coated bike lanes as well as left- and right-turning lanes with traffic signals and perhaps a six-second delay for cars. Build parking lots and garages for bicycles to decrease the overcrowding and make sidewalks more spacious and safer. Hopefully, these are good ideas that could become a project that cuts down on accidents, injuries, and violence.

Listen, everything will not be to everybody's satisfaction. For example, I hate spinach, but you may love it. Water does not mix with oil but all-purpose flour works well with both. There are many who do not agree that bicyclists should mingle with motorists; however, while we do not have to like them, we must learn to tolerate them. Just like we continue to learn about different cultures, lifestyles, how to live among wild, deadly animals, and to appreciate race relations, we need to come together to learn, understand, and appreciate the motorist-bicyclist relationships. No matter how much grief these suicidal bicyclists bring upon me, as a motorist, I must learn to accept and welcome them for they are a major factor and are here to stay. After all, it is all about human relations. Now if I see bicyclists on the expressway, I am the first to say, "It's not my fault if I run your ass over."

How about building an expressway for bicyclists? Oh, I forgot. The city never has any money. I just want bicyclists to be conscious that the dangers faced by them, pedestrians, and motorists are preventable. Not everyone is familiar with these roads. Besides the courageous there are many out-of-towners who might just be exploring different areas of the city. To protect people and prevent accidents, I think there need to be "no bicycling" signs posted throughout the city on dangerous roads as there are for large vehicles. I am sure there are bicycle-friendly cities throughout the United States and in countries across the seas that would not mind sharing their strategies and advice about how motorists and bicyclists can become good neighbors. Perhaps council members, bicycle advocates, and coalition groups in other countries could unite to establish rules for making the city streets accessible for both motorists and bicyclists. I hope my city can establish a good, decent, and healthy relationships and make the necessary adjustments for the safety of everyone on the road.

DRIVING DOWN THE street, I glance at my watch and noticed the time. I palm my fist with a slap and instantly get a migraine headache. Believe me when I tell you that I have moved heaven and earth in preparation for dealing with the tyrants that will board my vehicle. No matter how much I try to convince myself that the next day will be better, those little crumb snatchers prove me wrong. Right before I open my doors these goons and goblins crowd the streets as if there is a parade and abruptly stop the flow of traffic, regardless of the traffic lights. Bright red is a universal law that means stop, do not move. But to the walking dead, the light is always green. All of the cars, trucks, and jeeps begin honking their horns and yelling at them to get out of the street. Honking horns and yelling at them does not by any means make any of their bones tremble. It takes them one hour to cross a twenty-five-foot street, and they deliberately stop in front of your vehicle, look you in the face, give you major neck action while rolling their eyes, and then slowly walk off as if to say, "Bitch! I wish you would hit me."

The motorist reactions are of no use because they only increase their frustration. Over and over I have seen many motorists get out of their vehicles to assault and chase these little devils into hiding. There have been a few occurrences where their anger has gotten so out of control, they insult the crossing guards, who have nothing to do with these brats. If there is no discipline in the homes, and they are ignorant in the classrooms, what is a crossing guard suppose to do? It seems like everything associated with mayhem is all fun and games, one huge joke. I open my doors, and now all the chaos and the obnoxious behavior that had been taking place on the outside is polluting the inside of my vehicle. As soon as my doors open, the school kids fall on the steps, get trampled on, bump, trip, and fall onto the passengers who were already on the vehicle without saying "excuse me" or "I'm sorry." They seem to think that nobody should be in their way. Immediately, they become loud, rowdy, and rude. Due to the unbearable noise, most of my passengers exit the vehicle before their stops, and wait for the next bus or walk to where they need to be.

After only two minutes, I cannot combat with these idiots. So, do you know what I do, how I regain control of my vehicle? In situations like this, I live by the following motto: *I will completely fuck your day up before you fuck mine. I will shut this shit down! Nobody ain't going nowhere on this vehicle!* I pull over to the side, call headquarters and the police, shut my vehicle off, and open the doors. Hell, I even open the emergency roof tops and windows to help them make a speedy exit! Then I shout, "All for one, and one for all! Get the hell off! If any of you get on my vehicle tomorrow or thereafter and turn into a bunch of monkeys, I will stop my vehicle again and have the cops haul your asses away into your cages. I cannot stand your disrespectful asses!"

My adult passengers begin thanking me, and some try to pay me. Headquarters calls; I explain the crisis, and the cops come. Before the cops reach my vehicle, a few school kids stay on to apologize or plead their case. I do not want to hear it. The police finally arrive and poof! The misfits are gone.

These little creatures are thoughtless and pay no attention to their surroundings. I do not know who they thought I was or what they thought they were about to do. But on this day they found out who was in control and running the show. This next story is both sad and cruel, but for me and my passengers it turned out to be an ass kicking to a happy ending.

It was spring with lots of sunshine and pleasant weather. My vehicle, like many others, was scheduled to be at this high school. Once the high school let out, the kids rushed the buses and the terror began. When the kids were on board, I started on my regular route. At one stop, I picked up an elderly lady, perhaps in her eighties. She was approximately five feet, two inches tall and very thin, weighing less than one hundred pounds. She wore a set of mismatched clothes, including burgundy skirt; opaque, chalk-colored stockings, and multicolored flat shoes and held a gray pocketbook. She sat to my right in the very first seat. Once four of the teenage girls spotted the lady, their mouths turned into a deadly weapon. They ripped her apart! Two girls did the actual talking about the lady, and the other two laughed and made comments like "Y'all so wrong, y'all going to hell." They laughed and made fun of her mismatched clothing right to her face. They asked her questions such as, "Did you take a look at yourself before you left your house? You look like the joker in *Batman*," and then laughed. The lady was shaking and crying. Do you think they stopped? No, they continued to press on. About five minutes before I came to a major stop, the girls laughed and said, "Don't cry, old lady. We're not going to beat you up. We might push you down and take your money. Psych!"

I felt pure shame. Guilt-ridden questions of guilt kept replaying in my head. How could I allow these despicable teenage girls to humiliate and torment this daughter, sister, cousin, niece, mother, wife, grandmother, perhaps great-grandmother? Ninety-eight percent of the time I will call for help and kick them off of my vehicle. I had actually thrown students from this high school off of my bus twice before. What was preventing me from tossing them on their asses this time? My heart ached and sunk deeper and grew heavy as I cried for the elderly lady. My eyes filled with tears because I could not reach out to help her. It was as if this powerful force was inside me, holding me down. It seemed as if I were struggling against powerful gusts of wind. A voice repeatedly said to me, "Just keep driving."

I arrived at the stop where most of the passengers got out, and I get a new set of passengers. Ah, ha! This was where it got interesting. Two women, the same height and build of Tyler Perry's Madea, stepped onto my vehicle and said to the lady in a hurt tone while they took two of her grocery bags, "Nana! Nana! What happened? Why are you crying??" The passengers who were exiting through the rear doors stopped, turned around, and tried to grab themselves a seat. Then a guy appeared through the crowd and yelled, "These two skanks right here caused your nana to cry her whole ride." Then everybody on board jumped on the band wagon and said, "Yup, these two right here did it." One of the women helped their grandmother get off of the bus and sat her in the car that was parked in front. She told a man, who had a full beard and towered over her, "Babe, take Nana home and meet us at Blue Avenue." She returned to the bus and said, "Bitch! Now it's your turn to cry." Then the same guy yelled, "That's right! Wassup! Don't get scared now!" Then he told the Madea sisters every detail of the situation. I closed my doors, and the ones who were suppose to get off stayed on. The two sisters faced me and said," Do not pick up nobody until you get to Blue Avenue." I said, "You got it" and stepped on the gas.

The vehicle was so quiet you could hear a piece of cotton fall on the floor. The only thing I saw was one of the sisters grab one of the girls by her throat and head to the back of my vehicle. Then I heard the girl's scream, "No! I'm sorry!" Boom! Boom! Bop! Pow! Bam! Slam! It sounded like thunder and lightning aboard my vehicle. Some of the passengers were standing in the seats, and the aisles were jammed packed as I passed by all the transit stops. The coolest part of it all was that not a single passenger rung that bell when we got to each stop. Then I shouted, "Blue Avenue" and opened the doors. The first two people to leave through the back door were the two, now badly beaten, staggering teenage girls, who fell down onto the ground. The Madea sisters became instant heroines. The passengers began clapping their hands and thanking them as they stepped down off the vehicle. About three to four transit stops after Blue Avenue, I pulled over and parked the bus, got out of my seat, and went to the back. There was hair weave everywhere, blood on my back windows, and one broken chair. All I could say was, "Well, goddamn," which made the passengers burst out laughing. They told me the graphic details with delight, ending the story with, "Girl, you can have this damn job. There's no amount of money that they can offer me to do this damn job. God bless and be safe." The beat down of those teenage girls was the main topic of discussion until the very last passenger got off. The most amazing part is that two women cleaned the back of the bus with their own cleaning products. Once I reached the end of the line, my work day was over, and my vehicle smelled like a swimming pool. Luckily, no one passed out from the strong fumes. Back at the depot, the guys said, "What the hell happened on your vehicle? Someone drop a gallon of bleach?" I chuckled and said, "Yeah, something like that."

I did not contact headquarters or write up an incident report. As far as I was concerned, they got what they deserved. Furthermore, I was not a witness to the assaults. I wish every day that someone would kick people's teeth down their throats for their repulsive behavior. With the sigh of relief, I would say:

> Wow, I have had a smooth and relaxed day. My sit vehicle has some kick, all the buttons and controls are working, and it has not given me any problems. There are no doubled-parked cars blocking the flow of traffic. No one screamed in my ear, "Wait! You got a runner!" There were no accidents or detours. Passengers got on, sat down, and shut up. Conversations were low; some read a book or the paper or listened to their iPods, while others were just chillin', enjoying the ride. So yeah, I can sit back, show my choppers and happily say, "So far today has been a good day."

Aw, shit! Damn it! Damn it! Damn it! I spoke too soon! Here we go again with these ignorant school kids! Constant pushing, shoving, fighting, screaming, throwing objects, smoking weed, and even jumping out of the windows. And, oh my God, just hearing their conversations will cause you to quiver. Their language is so abusive and smutty, it will have the devil shit in his pants. You can depend on these little monsters to vandalize the vehicles every single day. They carve words in the windows, write on the seats, and trash the vehicles with junk food, bottles, cans, etc. They are amused by their disorderly behavior and believe that they are untouchable. They do not care who is watching or who they offend, and you had better not say a word to them. They are so corrupted their body language has an attitude: "Yeah, look at me. I said it. I done it, so what you gonna do about it?" They know no shame therefore have no self-respect.

It is like going to the movies and watching a freak show. Mass transit operators only have two heaven-sent, short months of freedom from these spooky little critters. Each summer, weeks seem to vanish; there are not enough hours in a day. Soon, what do you know? The freak show featuring the spooky little critters is back. The kids seem demoralized, lost, and socially inept. Whoever said you must wait until October 31 for Halloween needs to come to my part of town and ride the mass transit system. I am not the only one; a whole city of adults absolutely hate whenever kids are back in school and use the public buses because their rides have been transformed into the Halloween rollercoaster for ten long, brutal months. They do not know how to have a friendly and decent conversation. They have such unpleasant attitudes and intentionally take pleasure in inexcusable and disruptive behavior among their peers and adults and with other people's property. That is the main reason why mass transit operators do what we call a drive by: the school kids will be waiting at the transit stops, and a row of buses will zoom past them with fire in our tracks. The passengers understand; if they need that particular stop, I will let them off about fifty feet before or after. And if a vehicle does have school kids on board, people waiting at the stops will wave it on, shake their heads, and yell, "Hell, no! Keep going." Dealing with these school kids is equivalent to dealing with the pain of a toothache. Their behavior is dysfunctional, out of control, and too much trouble. All of their energy is pushed toward pissing people off and destroying property, day after day.

I have written a few complaints, as have many of my coworkers, about the bad occurrences school kids cause aboard mass transit vehicles. Every week it seems to get worse. But management has taken no preventive actions to stop their harmful behavior. They are not disciplined or held responsible for their damages. The authorities could have them do some type of weekend community services or fine their parents or guardians. I believe the transit system managers need to renegotiate their deal with the school board and come up with bright, new ideas on how to manage the madness.

I've noticed that the school kids' disruptive behavior has been in existence for many years. When I was a kid it was bad, and it still is. Why, after so many years, has no one has attempted to control these school kids when they are on public property? I am sure something can be done. Or is it that the transit system management does not care about anyone's safety? Just as long as money is being collected, they have no worries? You probably figure, how bad could it really be? The school kids only ride a few hours each day. Chuck it up and swallow it. I will tell you how bad it can get. As soon as they get on, I want them to get off. It is like being in a good, deep sleep, then being awakened by ambulance sirens, a sound that never goes away even when the ambulances are long gone. You try your hardest to regain that level of warmth and comfort and to rest your head, but you can't.

Then you become restless and begin twisting and turning your body every three seconds until after an hour you find the relaxing position. Then the clock alarm goes off, and the beast breaks out. You are totally frustrated. You have been robbed of your rest.

Or imagine being invited to a Thanksgiving dinner that starts at 5 p.m. A month prior, you have informed your family that you are taking a long drive to spend Thanksgiving Day with a friend so you will see everyone the day after the holiday. You are so hungry as you walk toward the friend's home and up their steps with turkey, stuffing, gravy, and candied yams on your mind. All the while you are thinking, "I hope they won't have everyone standing around, holding hands for a twenty-minute grace. I mean, really, bless the food, thank the Lord, and eat!" Once I was inside their house, they apologetically revealed, "We have no food. I would have called but we arrived here five minutes before you did." I did not know what to think or what to feel. I looked around, and it did not seem as if their home had been burglarized. I asked with a puzzled look, "So what happened?" Long story short: their dogs ate the food. The two large Rottweiler dogs were in the basement while their owners prepared the table with all the food and trimmings. One of them visited a neighbor's home to see their newborn baby while the other drove to the airport to pick up their parents. When they arrived home, they found that their two well-trained, hungry, 160-pound, muscular dogs—the ones they claim listen to their every command, can have their bowls removed while they are feasting without growling, and can be walked without a leash—had broken through the basement door, jumped up on the table, and eaten the food. Were they crazy? They were cooking all day and tasting food in front of their dogs, but didn't think that they would notice and understand what was happening. They could smell the food and knew their owners were about to devour that food without them. They did not even eat their full bowl of dry dog food that day! Hell, no, they didn't eat it, especially after seeing what they saw! That should have given those fools a clue that the dogs wanted to eat our Thanksgiving food.

I was still hungry. My mouth was now dry and my stomach roaring like a lion. And now I was angry too. They could see the horror in my face. Then they calmly stated, "So to replace our Thanksgiving dinner, we ordered Chinese food, and our parents went to pick it up. We are so sorry. Please accept our apology and stay." I'd just had Chinese food the day before. I didn't want any damn Chinese food on Thanksgiving night! Oh, you do not know how badly I wanted to wring their necks, scream, and call them every foul and foolish name in Richard Pryor's dictionary. But after that long drive, Chinese food had to do. Of course, it did not compensate for my missed turkey and stuffing dinner, because that is what I had my mind set on, but it curbed my hunger.

The annoyance, frustrations, and anger I experienced on those occasions are the same emotions my coworkers, passengers, and I feel when we have to deal with school kids. The transit operator's question is, "Why must we pick up these school kids who act like howling wolves? Why didn't the transit authority make a deal with the SPCA, wild life society, pest patrol, or the state prisons to pick them up? This seems more like a job for them. Why can't the city's school district provide transportation for its own kids? For sure, the more public vehicles accommodate school kids, the more money the city pulls in. I assume that in return for fewer school buses, the school district saves bundles of dollars and gets a percentage of the earnings of the mass transit system authority. Sounds like a double plus to me. They both profit. It seems like there must be money floating around somewhere if the superintendant of public schools is able to get a pay increase and make six figures. Maybe somebody can grab that floating money and do some good deeds, such as increase the school teachers' pay and put arts and extracurricular activities back into these public schools. It is just a thought. That is another topic for another book and another author. Whether or not there is such as deal between the mass transit authority and the city school district, there is a need to put all those hundreds of yellow school buses, currently sitting in parking lots, back in service. If there is an existing deal, use the transit system money to repair those school buses fast! When I drive under stressful conditions, it is not safe for me, the passengers, bystanders, and other motorists. And the teenagers' reign of terror aboard the mass transit vehicles is unfair to the thousands of men and women who also ride. Whether they are riding one block away or to the end of the transit line, these people deserve an untroubled ride.

Many people take public transportation to save money and avoid paying high gas prices. It definitely beats searching and paying for parking. Some passengers do not want to fight the hustle and bustle of rush-hour traffic. Mass transit takes them exactly where they need to be, give or take a few blocks. Whatever their reasons, I thank them all because I would not have a job without their loyalty. However, I am entirely certain that none of them expects a torturous ride. People do not board the vehicles saying, "Okay kids, listen up! Today I want you to give me the worst headache of my life. I want my head to pound, with my eyes bulging out of my head, veins popping, and my mouth foaming. I want to be covered in spit balls, hit with a bat in my stomach, and have a foot up my ass. And oh, please do not forget to throw a thirty-gallon bag of dirt on me as you get off. I appreciate it. You're the best. I love you guys. Same time tomorrow?" It would be such a pleasant ride if they could discuss their family vacations, summer jobs, or the latest movie; instead, they fight or talk about sex and drugs.

WHATEVER HAPPENED TO a kid just being a kid? Living freely without worries and enjoying life? Giggling; laughing; playing double dutch, jacks, ball, video games, and hopscotch; going down the slide? What happened to sitting on the steps, licking on some ice cream, sucking on a lollipop, and chewing grape bubble gum and blowing a bubble the size of your head that bursts all over your face?

Whatever happened to being courteous and respectful in the presence of adults? What happened to going to skating rinks, bowling, bicycling, or to parties without drama? What happened to going to the beach, amusement parks, the mall, the movies, and grandma's house? What happened to their dreams of being a teacher, a nurse, an artist, a movie star? Kids still have dreams, do they not? What happened to knowing what is right? Whatever happened to the sense of wrong? What happened to wanting to make your parents proud? What happened to wanting to be just like mom and dad and to do better in life than they did? What happened to honor and respect and the days when kids listened and did not talk back? Do these words no longer exist and hold value for today's youth?

Whatever happened to fear? You know the fear that creates tears, goose bumps, and body tremors, "Ooh! I'm gonna tell your mom!" Or "Ooh, you're gonna get it now!" What happened to the look mothers gave that made kids pee on themselves and stumble off in the opposite direction? Remember when just the sound of a father's breathing made kids wish they were not alive at that moment? That was my fear factor! What happened to the word "try": when I get knocked down I will get back up; to "tried": I got knocked down, but I got back up; to "trying": I continue to get knocked down, and I will continue to get back up. Whatever happened to love? Are these kids not being raised properly? Haven't they been shown true affection from parents or guardians, who care for them unconditionally; help and encourage their kids in times of crisis; are involved in and show interest in their kids' lives, without criticizing or being judgmental; and hug, kiss, and simply say "I love you"?

What happened to kids wanting to get an education? I am not referring to young people deciding not to go to college but to their decisions to drop out of high school. This is a total outrage. What is possibly going through their minds to make dropping out of high school seem like a good idea? How is dropping out of high school a choice? What life-threatening family crisis could cause so many kids to give up on educating themselves? Are they being bullied in school; suffering from peer pressure, insecurity issues, low self-esteem, or depression; or dealing with major personal issues at home, such as alcoholic parent(s) or guardians; sexual, physical, mental, or drug abuse; a party house; eviction notices; or death? These conditions are extremely traumatic at any age, and I understand how they can hinder concentration or lead to learning disabilities. Parents and educators must join together to help these kids, and let them know help is available. These kids may need to speak confidentially to someone who can help them put their lives in order and back on the right track.

Of course, there are a lot of kids who do not care to go to school and would rather gamble with their lives. They are dropping out of school at alarming rates because they want to grow up fast. They actually believe that they are missing out on life's pleasures by staying in school and receiving an education. They have this stupid notion that school will not prepare them for life, and they know that they can always choose to return to school and receive their GEDs. But right now, they care only about the money. That is the reason these kids lose interest and become bored with school. They rebel against the idea of educating themselves, against their parents and others who care and want to help by speaking to them about their life decisions. Then they begin to hang with the wrong crowd. Some become strippers and exotic dancers, work at low or underpaid jobs, become drug abusers, and become neighborhood corner boys who are a waste of soap and have sex with male and female drug addicts. They look at it as taking the easy way out. It's not really about needing any brain power. It is all about parties and having a good time.

But it is about having an education to achieve your dreams and accomplish your goals. Being a well-rounded person, the best person you can be, and embracing life with open arms shows that you are not afraid of taking risks. You showcase who you are by loving yourself, having dignity, and living your life to the fullest. And believing that having an education was, is, and will always be the only correct answer to tomorrow confirms that knowledge is infinite. Dropping out of school does not bring happiness, only sorrow. This lack of self dignity and not wanting to get an education is a slap in the face to those who had to protest to be recognized, fight to succeed, and did not have the abundance of opportunities available then as kids have today. The journeys that took place before your time took people from hiding and sneaking to learn how to read a word on a page to scrambling to read the first line on a page to struggling to read a full page to striving to receive an education. And still many of you simply do not care about yourselves or about putting forth the effort toward receiving an education. Why? It is like you are throwing the history book documenting our very existence into the incinerator, with ashes scattering in the wind and disintegrating in the air. It is a disgrace to our ancestors who struggled to pave their way in America and this world, bleeding confidence and determination for a noble future.

There is nothing stopping young people from wanting and choosing to become fortunate in this world. Every one of those kids is living in the land of opportunity. I read an article in a magazine a while ago, and there was a graph comparing levels and effects of education between poverty-stricken black and white kids. The article said that 60 or 70 percent of poverty-stricken white kids are at or above standard levels of education compared to only 20 percent of poverty-stricken black kids. I know children who are in desperate situations and go to the so-called underfunded public schools. And may I proudly add that they are respectful and smart, and their report cards and citywide test grades met or exceeded standard levels, which prove their abilities to succeed in impossible circumstances. You must swim to reach the land of opportunity. And swimming requires you to use all the muscles in your body that were never used before. Kids must stimulate that big old muscle in their heads called the brain. It is built to handle hard work. So it is important to put the brain to good usage! Protect it, work it, exercise it, play with it, build a relationship with it, just do something creditable with it. Staying in school and receiving an education is the best opportunity to achieve a productive life. Kids should study three to four hours every day. If they can text, Facebook, tweet, watch music videos, download music, and whatever else that does not help anyone get an education, they can study.

My advice to young people: If you do not know how to prepare yourself to study, open your mouths and ask for help. Your teachers are there to help and tutor you with difficult subjects.

Take advantage of the opportunity presented to you and rely on your teachers. Ask, ask, ask, and continue asking questions and for help if you do not understand the work rather than become frustrated, which often leads to inattentiveness, anger, and dropping out of school.

This is such a misguided era for this new generation of kids. Some of the music being produced presents false portrayals of people and fails to show that the so-called glamorous ghetto life is short-lived. A couple of these songs and raps repeat the same phrases with a different singer: the goal is to make baller money, get lots of sex, buy material things, and do drugs. Quite a few of these artists have no personality or flavor, nor do their songs leave anything to the imagination. This type of music seems to say that a person has not reached his full potential in life without indulging in those four elements. Kids' minds are clouded with so much negative hype about the underworld that they too believe they are forced to live in hell. I beg to differ. I am a firm believer in no pain, no gain. In other words, no one will give you anything for free and nothing worth having will come easily. That is not how this world works. You've got to give to get and produce to get paid. In other words, you have to get a job and be productive to earn money. As my great-grandmother, God bless her soul, told me on my thirteenth birthday, "The only responsibilities you have until you're grown and on your own is to learn, eat, sleep, and poop. You are not missing out on anything that life has to offer. Please do me a favor and remain a kid as long as you can, because once you become an adult, it ain't nothing but a big ole headache from paying bills, men, kids, and more men." She didn't lie!

Somehow, somewhere, however, these kids got lost. It is very sad, going forward in the twenty-first century, to see, hear, and read about young people not caring about themselves or having any ambitions. How did we lose these kids? Who failed these kids? Who is to blame? Who should be held accountable for their behavior? Does anyone really care? Have people thrown up their hands, saying, "I have my education, a good job, and home. As long as those kids do not come to my part of town, I'm cool." Is the word out on the streets: "to hell with them, let them rot"? Are parents no longer actively involved with their children's lives, specifically their education, friends, household rules, and discipline? Are parents scheduling regular family time to discuss the day's events, eating together, visiting family and friends, and attending parent-teacher conferences and community meetings?

It is not easy being a single parent. I have had to iron out quite a few difficulties and challenges with my teenage son. For instance, sometimes, he feels as though I am too hard on him. Instead of asking for my help, Mr. I'll Do It My Way will avoid me, which always leads to disappointment. He is at that age where he is a tad rebellious; however, I soon bring him back to reality. It is a characteristic part of growing up. Regardless of the difficulty of the situation, I am his parent, and I have always, am still and will continue to involve myself in every aspect of his life, nourishing him to become the decent, respectful young man that he is by staying on top of his education, disciplining him when needed. Having a good, healthy, strong mother-and-son bond is important to both of us. I need to stay connected to him and stand firm and strong regarding our family values so that I will not lose him to the world. I want him to know that his mother's love is all his and that I will not hurt him. Sometimes my son get tired of me constantly drilling him about cleaning, studying, and the wicked behavior of people, or he becomes frustrated at my demands. Yoo hoo. Over here. Guess what? He knows that I do not give a flying jackass about how he—the child who I solely provide for by working; paying all of the bills; buying all the food household items, clothes shoes, and athletic wear; cooking; cleaning; allowing his friends into my home, paying for multiple activities, and all of the other stuff that comes along with good parenting—feels about how I teach him about the ways of life. I am the parent, a.k.a. the boss. In my home, I have no tolerance for a funky-talk-to-the-back-of-my-head child. That will be the day that I call the cops and tell them to come to my home with a body bag because I've just committed a murder! Unruliness gets corrected in my home immediately! My child was corrected as a toddler; there is no reason for me to stop because he is a now teenager. He needs me more than ever. There is no such thing as a slap on the hand. There is no such thing as his parent turning over his or her responsibilities to someone else. You know what I am talking about. There are parents who will tell their kids:

1. "I will tell your father. Let him deal with you."

2. "For your next school year, I'm sending you to your grandparent's house."
3. "You're fifteen now, damn near grown. If you got a problem with the people I bring home, you can leave."
4. "You are too much trouble, and I don't got to take this shit. I am handing your ass over to the state. Let them raise you."
5. "You know what? I've had it! Boarding school, here he [or she] comes! I'm done with your ass! I don't got to see you until weekends and holidays. And that is if only I want to come and pick you the fuck up!"

In all five of these scenarios, the kids are the ones who have to leave. They are also jaw-dropping moments that seem to come from the movie *Jackass*. For me, these acts are as delusional as my teenage child standing toe to toe with me, waving his hands in my face, and with a "whatever" attitude saying, "I don't care. Just hurry up and say what it is that you gotta say so I can go." It is confusing for me to try and grasp this type of situation, although I hear similar things daily from my passengers and people that I know personally.

And I do not know how the reversal of roles came about, with the child being the parent and the parent being the child, but it has happened. I have taught my child what I have been taught and also believe. You too are a person and are just as important as an adult. Kids have feelings and should be heard, but it is all about how you do it. Now, a kid can express his or her thoughts, ideals, and opinions to any adult but must learn to express them politely.

However, kids today question their parents' authority with attitudes that seem to say "who in the hell do you think you're talking to?" And the parents submissively explain their every answer. Here are a few typical scenarios:

1. Parent: "You cannot have that phone."
   Child: "Why not? Well I'll just ask my aunt."

2. Parent: "You're not wearing that."
   Child: "Why not? You didn't buy it!"

3. Parent: "This weekend you're not going anywhere."
   Child: "Man whatever! Watch me!"

4. Parent: "Clean your room now."
   Child: "Why? You don't sleep in here."

5. Parent: "Take the trash out."
   Child: "I will once I finish playing my game."

My child has tried my patience with an edgy tone, as I think all children have done to their parents. It is called the, "I'm getting too damn old for you to be bossing me around" tone. It is a way to get parents to recognize their growth by saying:

> Look at me. I use deodorant, am able to distinguish colors, and can use the microwave. I'm just as tall as you, if not taller. I'm not a little kid anymore

> at whom you can snap your finger, and I'll jump. I'm tired of doing all of the chores—cleaning the house, walking the dog, and raking the leaves. I'm a teenager, and I have a life. It's about hanging out, being stupid, and getting into a little trouble.

Kids will try to search for their parents' weaknesses, to see what they can and cannot get away with. This is to get a feeling of how long they can agitate their parents' nerves before they snap. My son, however, has failed to repeat such a behavior. He understands that I do not play those types of games. When I tell him to do something, he does it without back talking or complaining. He can explain the meaning of the following phrases: poke it out, I'll bust it open; roll them, I'll shut them; suck them, I'll Mack-truck 'em; put your hands up, I'll kill you. In other words, do not bite the hand that feeds you for God made the backhand for a purpose. Allowing your child to stand toe to toe with you and have a word with you is total humiliating and an insult to your existence as a parent. It is why today's youth do not respect their teachers or any other adults or property or the law, because these parents allow their children to spit into their faces and walk away without any repercussions.

Shamefully, these are situations that many parents throw themselves into. Morality is a lesson that must be taught from infancy through adolescence. That grip on your child should feel like a choke hold: stiff, tight, and leaving him gasping for air. I am not talking about being an overprotective or abusive parent—then the child would not be able to breathe—but to raising your child with a set of rules, whether he is an infant, toddler, young girl or boy, or a teenager graduating from high school. As I tell my son, it is my duty to get the hell on his nerves. If that means voluntarily giving him advice; talking to him about drugs, sex, and everyday life; keeping track of his whereabouts; asking about his day; checking on his homework; telling him to do his chores, stop texting at the dinner table, go to bed, and "no," all I can say is, "too bad!" My child has no choice; there ain't a damn thing he can do about it.

The arrogance of these teenagers has a stench that can be noted five miles away. When I was growing up, talking back to my parents, grandparents, aunts, uncles, teachers, or any adult or questioning their authority was not a thought. If the thought were spoken, that would be the day the paramedics asked, "What train wreck was she in?" We kids were told that if any adult said or did any wrong to us, we should never be afraid to tell our parents. The parents will take care of those adults. As a child, I graciously accepted every no because I was scared for my life! In the 1970s and 1980s, people did not joke around about life's lessons. I knew not to act as if I were ear hustling (trying to overhear someone's conversation)! When grown folk started a conversation, they did not have to tell me to leave the room, I knew to get out of sight. See, when I was about four inches tall, my family showed me what they would do to me—showed me all the handmade devices, gadgets, and tools (six braided and knotted belts that were tied or sewn together and looked ten feet long) and explained how each one worked—if I ever interfered in grown-ups' business. I did not feel comfortable joining in grown-up conversations in my family until I was almost thirty years old. Today, I am almost forty years old and I will not cuss or reveal my wild side to my older relatives. Yes, I am grown and can do and say anything I please, but I was loved and raised in a moral manner and would never disrespect my family because I am an adult. I have been involved in many discussions on this topic, and everyone is in agreement that kids today do not believe they possess the power, strength, and ability to succeed in this world.

Kids are the future. There are children walking the streets right now with the intelligence of Thomas Jefferson and Albert Einstein. One of them could be the person who discovers the cures for uterine and other various cancers. He or she could be the one who discovers a cure for spinal injury paralysis or a method for regrafting skin cells perfectly after third-degree burns. He or she might be the one who discovers the cure for HIV/AIDS or syphilis, genital herpes, and genital warts. Kids are drowning; they want to be a part of something but do not know how to break away from peer pressure. Nowadays the "in thing" is to be corrupted, get wasted, have unprotected sex, buy gear, and be a dummy in school. Their perception on life is head-on backward. They are more concerned about "this minute" than about the future, act strictly on impulse, and would rather be rewarded among their peers by being crowned the "top gangster for the day" than worry about the risks of retaliation and being locked up.

And what do these school kids who were born in the 1990s know about the white man holding them back? That kind of stupid talk comes from bitter adults, weighed down in misery and blaming their laziness, faults, failures, and ignorance on the "white man." That statement is as worn out as a porn star's body and as dead as bodies in the morgue. It is not fair for adults to instill that slave mentality into school kids because they failed to take advantage of the fruits of life. There is no segregated education. Today, all races can and do attend the same schools. Now, I have read articles, overheard conversations, and taken part in discussions regarding poverty-stricken neighborhood schools that do not have updated textbooks. Is that true? Is that really the reason why so many kids are rated below-standard illiteracy levels or are they just not studying? For example, four young kids living in poverty attend their neighborhood school, which is rated one of the worst in the city. These four kids do not come from a background of scholars. All they know are high-school dropouts, drug addicts, and corner boys, and their single mother is on welfare. But this mother knows she does not want her children running in the streets; she wants them to go to college. Every day, after school, these children are in the house studying their lessons. These four kids attend one of the worst schools in the city, but they are honor students, and each one of them earned high scores on the citywide standardized tests. Four kids living in poverty; again I ask, "Is it true that schools in poverty-stricken neighborhoods are not taught the same curricula and do not have updated books? Or are the kids just not putting in the time to study?"

No white man ever came into my neighborhood and pointed a gun at my head, my sister's head, or my son's head and forced us to act a fool in school or drop out and live the fast life of the streets. No white man threatened our lives if we did not vandalize the property of the mass transit system authority or become deranged idiots in the streets. Now, you ask yourself who is to blame. These school kids are living in the land of chance and opportunity. What people need to do is rise up and get past race as the reason they continue to hold themselves back. In reality, these school kids are the generation who will soon be in charge of the world's affairs. It is our requirement as citizens of the United States of America to save our future leaders and bring them out of the darkness and help them with their social skills. Sadly there are a good number of people who will not change. They need to find some inner peace for that is the key to happiness.

Slowly but surely, neighborhood libraries are going out of business and are being taken out of our communities. The rate of failure of high-school dropouts is so significantly high and widespread, I heard a radio news report that stated that some locations in the United States plan to discontinue the twelfth grade. The rationale behind this idea is, "What is the purpose of funding a senior class if there are not enough students to fill a classroom? It is a waste of money." Guess what? Since kids do not want to stay in school, there are buildings being built to house them and land available for their final rest—prisons and graveyards. Unfortunately a lot of our kids will travel down the devil's road of the doomed. People who really care about the future of these young people can only meet them halfway. Parents are the ones who have to see that their kids grow up to be decent human beings.

I believe that a large percentage of these school kids are illiterate and have mental issues or illnesses. Just hearing them conversing with one another is so sad. Day in and day out, my ears hear conversations filled with pain and hurt. Instead of thinking of how to make a situation better, these kids become enraged and filled with thoughts of revenge and resentment. And to hell with school! Right now, this minute, getting an education is a negative. If school can't show them how to make money now, how to get rich quick, it is a waste of time. They say: "School is not for me." "I can't do two more years in school." "I'm tired and sick of school." "School bores me; all I do is sleep." "Forget about a cap and gown; I need money." Despite their young ages, their lives are soap operas filled with drama. In my opinion, a lot of these kids probably would be satisfied with just getting a job anywhere or becoming career criminals, sticking people up and in many cases killing their victims for their hard-earned cash or material things. I know a change for the better is going to come. You must go through the dark clouds and stormy weather to see the sun. For a couple of years, it has been very cloudy.

If these school kids are diagnosed with mental problems, I think a rehabilitation program is greatly needed to help them with their issues and provide them with the proper care. There must be involvement on every level possible, beginning with the parents, who can provide inside information on their children's development and character. They also can help obtain neighborhood funding for schools and recreational centers with family therapists, psychologists, social workers, behavioral and anger-management therapists, counselors, mentors, community leaders, and preachers as well as programs like drama therapy, mental-health therapy, drug rehab, group therapy, hypnotherapy, etc. Also, there should be programs in which mass transit operators can speak to school kids about rules, safety, and etiquette on public vehicles. Police officers, prison guards, and correctional officers could speak about the consequences of violent behavior and describe the reality of what could happen to their young, soft bodies in prison if they do not turn their lives around. Because right now these kids think going to prison is some type of badge of honor, but it is not cool and kids need to know the real deal about prison life.

Do kids really want to talk about sex? Because sex is their number one featured topic of conversation, one that they have no shame about broadcasting loudly and in public. Okay, then, let's talk about sex. Do they know about the dangers and death sentences that can result from risky sexual behavior? I have a message and a few tips for the ones who believe mass transit vehicles are the places for disclosing all of their trifling sex stories: the next time you get onto my vehicle, I'm going to drive full speed and crash into a gas station to blow you up. You do not have to be a junky or a prostitute to contract sexually transmitted diseases (STDs). Nor is AIDS solely a gay person's disease. So, let's talk about sex. The most common STDs are Chlamydia, genital warts, genital herpes, gonorrhea, herpes, HIV/AIDS, and syphilis. Let's talk about sex and take a trip to the clinic and get tested for STDs. Then let's talk about sex some more and see how many school kids will boldly stand and proudly shout out their results to everyone aboard the bus. Let's laugh and announce to everyone on board that the doctor said, "Yes, you've got the top five Cs: contagious, contaminated, crabs, the clap, and cooties!" You are now classified as that same type of dirty person who gets infected with STDs, that junkie, that hooker. Let's talk about sex and learn what certain STDs visually look like on human flesh.

Yeah, let's talk about how STDs do not discriminate according to gender, age, title, race, religion, weight, body odor, or wealth. According to the Centers for Disease Control and Prevention (CDC) as well as my family doctors, STDs can infect and be transmitted to an unborn baby and a newborn baby as easily as to a person who is one hundred years old. Yes, this means that you, your mother, your father, and the people you know, care for, and love can become infected. Let's talk about sex, about the diseases that have no cure, such as genital herpes, genital warts, gonorrhea (depending on the amount of internal or permanent damage), syphilis (depending on which stage it is in), and HIV/AIDS. However, there are medications and treatments that can keep outbreaks at a minimum, enable you to live a normal lifestyle, and prolong your lives, but that is it.

Let's talk about sex, about how to prevent yourselves from becoming a statistic. The methods of transmission for STDs include oral, vaginal, and anal sex with an infected person. You become infected with STDs when you have unprotected sex, exchange blood, or share needles with an infected person. It is impossible to look at a person and determine that he or she is infected. You are unable to see, touch, taste, smell, hear, or feel any STDs. You can prevent yourselves from becoming infected by using latex condoms with spermicide, the right size so they will not slip off or break and consistently to reduce or prevent transmission. It has been documented in pamphlets by the CDC, articles that I have read, TV commercials, and comments from my family doctors that you can contract genital herpes, genital warts, and syphilis while using condoms. You also can transmit genital herpes and genital warts even if you don't have any outbreaks, signs, or symptoms of the disease. With genital herpes, genital warts, and syphilis, transmission can result from direct skin contact because a condom simply cannot cover all the areas of the body where rashes and sores can develop. Depending on the stage of syphilis and early detection of gonorrhea, these STDs can be cured. Protect yourself and your hands when dealing with people who have blood, a cut, and sores on their bodies.

Of course the most effective way to stay clear and clean is abstinence, voluntarily refraining from having sex. There are many excellent reasons to refrain from sex: being unemotionally prepared, to prevent an unwanted pregnancies or unwanted STDs, due to religion or marriage, or because someone is unsuitable. If you are a virgin, hold your head up high and be proud. Do not allow the pressures of society to influence you to give up your virginity. Keep yourselves abreast of the latest developments in sex education. And if you are not a virgin but are in a monogamous relationship, practicing safe sex, or have chosen celibacy, I respectfully tip my hat to you to say thank you for your good sense of self respect and strong consistency of will power.

The only way to know for sure if you are infected is to get tested. There should be a free day, week, or month across the country to "take your child to the free clinic or doctor to be tested for STDs and HIV/AIDS." Hell, it seems like the only other time people go to the clinic is to get an exam to play sports, have a baby, or to get an abortion. This is just an idea that I am suggesting to parents and guardians. Schools, community services, and recreational centers could have open houses with nurses and doctors to conduct the tests as they do with blood drives, especially given the increasing numbers of teen pregnancies and STDs among teenagers. Who knows, maybe this could bring about change, with people becoming educated and being more tuned into their own health and helping to stop the epidemic of so many STDs and HIV/AIDS within our communities.

Nonetheless, there are teenagers who are infected with HIV/AIDS. And these same infected teenagers are participating in middle schools, high schools, and contact sports. Yes, I know this is a chilling thought as well as an uncomfortable position for a parent to imagine. But is not protecting your children part of being a good, responsible parent? For me, safety is the number one concern in sports. Having a strong healthy heart and a negative HIV/

AIDS status report are important medical issues that should be a serious consideration a child's physical examination. Imagine your child had a heart condition or any medical health issues. I have known a few parents who are overlooking their child's medical conditions just so the children can play sports. This degree of a situation cannot depend on a gut feeling, an aching heart, or a trivial-question game. These parents know that they are wrong for allowing their children to participate in certain sports. Their known medical conditions are being juggled with the stupidity and selfishness of the very adults these kids depend on for protection and call Mom and Dad. However, ignoring the problem, many parents psych themselves up and say, "What the hell. He'll [or she'll] be okay. These kids are young and strong. Let them play." Two scenarios:

1. Your teenage child is playing sports and then all of a sudden collapses on the court and lies in critical condition or instantly dies. Before, you had the opportunity to explain to your child that you would do anything in the world to keep him happy, and there is nothing better than to see him play sports. But due to "your medical condition and what it can do to you, I love you too much to have you suffer." But now your world has flipped upside down, and you are devastated, wracked with guilt about what you had known all along. And you cry, "Please God, not my baby."
2. Your teenage child who is HIV-negative is competing in a contact sport with an HIV-positive teenager. The other teen ager, his parents, school, neighborhood recreational centers,

> and other sponsors of sporting activities are clueless about the child's medical status. A tiny drip of blood from a cut on his arm is transmitted to another player. Your teenage child is now HIV-positive.

Any child with a serious medical condition should not be allowed to play certain sports. Under these same conditions, what would the professional sports leagues do? For example, one young adult has the dream of becoming a pro athlete. This person is a star athlete who has been diagnosed with chronic elbow pain. Will a professional team sign this person knowing that over time this condition will cause long-term pain and will be hard to manage? Will the professional league knowingly sign an HIV-positive athlete or allow him to continue playing? I believe the answer would be no. Given the amount of money they are paying them, they want healthy, young, strong, and energetic athletes who can bring more fans and more money into the league. And if the athlete's medical condition is critical, he is likely to take the time off to heal or retire.

Why not apply similar rules to the teenage athletes? It is unsafe and unfair to have a child with a critical medical condition participate in certain sporting activities. With the growing rate of teenage pregnancies, teenagers with STDs, and teenagers who are HIV-positive, do you think that I am being unreasonable, or am I just keeping up to date on the facts? Am I crazy and cruel, or am I connected to reality and have major concerns? Am I crushing a child's dreams or creating other possibilities in life? I surely would not want to be that parent under those circumstances, having my soul eaten away by "if only." I will repeat, these tests (heart screenings, HIV/AIDS) should be part of a child's annual physical examination. This is a major issue. We parents must help stop occurrences that might hurt our children. We should protest, sign petitions, and send letters to city council members until there is a law passed requiring these tests before children participate in sports. In personal, hard-hitting situations like this, I am quite sure it will be very hard for many kids as well as parents to even consider my point of view. Nonetheless, I am 100 percent on board for the testing of our teenagers because I am sure many of them are unaware about their medical condition. In today's world, I am only trying to wake these kids up, educate them, and save their lives. Knowing the facts of a situation, parents must do the right thing by choosing the correct answer.

For example, your four-year-old is crying from scratching the red marks on her body. You take her to see the pediatrician, who says she is allergic to popcorn, her favorite food. It is Saturday, and your child is sitting on the floor enjoying the cartoons. She pops the question, "Can I have some popcorn?" Hmm, what should you do? Tell your child, "Yes. But instead of giving you a big bowl of popcorn, I'll give you a sandwich bag full. This small amount will not make you scratch." Or do you say, "Sweetie, I want to talk to you first. Remember when you were crying and scratching your arms? That didn't feel too good, did it? Well, remember the nice doctor who gave you two lollipops? She knows a lot about your body. She said the scratching that made you cry and feel really, really bad came from eating popcorn. So, to stop you from crying and feeling bad, I cannot give you any popcorn." How many parents are guilty of dismissing the doctor's orders? Parents are the decision makers and we must do right by our kids because they learning from our example—watching what we do not think they see, remembering what we do not know they saw, and repeating what we did not expect them to hear.

There are school kids who think they can make it in this world without guidance, who think they have experienced life and therefore know everything about it. They don't want to hear the truth from wiser, more experienced, knowledgeable folk and have a snappy, crude response for everything someone says. But nothing good and worth having will enter their lives until they make themselves good and worth having. All of the anger issues, attitude problems, dramas, conflicts, and various other negative feelings and emotions could be invested into a more positive life changing and successful careers. For instance, those of you who constantly get into fights could enlist in the armed forces or become a fight instructor—boxing, kick boxing, self defense, martial arts; perhaps this could land you a job in a gym, the secret service, or the police force. We all know the type who loves to keep controversy escalating and gossip about everybody, including their mommas, the drama queens a.k.a. chicken heads: attend a performing arts school; become a radio personality, news reporter, a journalist, an author, director, play writer, poet, a comedian; do something and get a life! Trust me, there are jobs for you. For all the talk you do about sex, find a specialty in the medical field; become a health teacher, a sex therapist, a nurse, an obstetrician, a gynecologist, or a urologist. The wannabe international business dealers, the drug dealers—a.k.a. corner boys—can deal in non–life-threatening businesses, such as real estate, financial advising, negotiation, banking, advertising, marketing, claims adjusting, insurance sales, engineering, and science and math education. Those of you who must have the latest fashions, become a fashion consultant, fashion stylist, fashion designer, costume designer, fashion buyer for a department store, fashion writer/critic, fashion editor, or fashion marketer. Fascinated by lip gloss and keeping your hair tossed and your makeup flawless? It's all about the face! Become a dentist; be a makeup artist, hair stylist, barber, dermatologist, model, or cosmetic surgeon.

Tired of the game? Then stop playing. You can change your life around; learn about the government and become a political figure, a teacher, preacher, a life coach, a lawyer, or a judge. Think you are skillful? Your hands got that magic touch? Become a massage therapist, musician, carpenter, mechanic, painter or sculptor, civil engineer, or potter. They say that everyone has a wild side, so the animal lovers can volunteer at the local animal shelters; become a pet groomer or trainer; learn to make pet toys, food, safety devices, or care products; or become a veterinarian, zoologist, or scientist. To the devoted competitors and die-hard sport fanatics: study sports medicine; physical therapy; athletic training; sports reporting, analysis, or writing; sports commentary; photography; event planning; stadium and sports facility management; refereeing; or coaching. Who loves colorful flowers; beautiful butterflies; the soft sand and the cool summer breeze of the beach; mesmerizing colors of gold, red, and orange tree leaves; untouched snow covering the streets; and the dazzling dancing stars in the heavens? My guess would be those who love nature and being outdoors. Engage your creative vision by creating jaw-dropping and fabulous properties; become a landscape designer, groundskeeper, property developer, florist, horticulturist, nature photographer, astrologer, marine biologist, lifeguard, wildlife conservationist, tourist guide, travel agent, travel writer, captain of a ship, or an airline pilot.

Attention, school kids: turn your negatives into positives. Your negativity will stop you from becoming a successful force in life. Nobody wants to hire an angry person to represent his workplace. I would want to hire someone who has ambition and goals in life and shows that he has a good work ethic. Be bright, be strong, and learn to think for yourselves. I know peer pressure is difficult to overcome. But you must challenge your inner being and know that you can do better. You kids must rise up, break away from the nonsense, walk in the opposite direction, and not look back. Concentrate on building a relationship with yourself and begin to love yourself. Once you regain confidence and have that loving friendship with yourself, then you will be able to respect human nature. You do have a choice, and the choice is all yours. Believe me when I say, there is such a thing as being drama free, happy, and living a good life.

None of you kids are any different from me. I grew up in a one-parent household, have been introduced to drugs countless times, have crack heads in my family, and had to deal with peer pressure. I also had a chip on my shoulder, but mine was not directed toward people but toward achieving goals in life. My attitude was, *I ain't letting nothing stop me from getting mine*. "Mine" pertained to having a good paying job and being a home owner in a decent middle-class neighborhood, with or without a college education. Even though college did not work out for me, there was never a question that I would not find a good paying job. I challenged myself to see if I could get the dream jobs that I wanted, and I did. As a child, my dream jobs were to work for the airlines, the best insurance company, and to become a mass transit operator. Every job did good by me, especially with the hourly wages. My dream jobs allowed me to travel, provided great benefits, helped me raise my child and become a homeowner in a pleasant, middle-class neighborhood. Best of all, I am not crammed in a cubicle, loaded with piles of paperwork, with a supervisor looking over my shoulders and cluttering more work atop of the existing mountain.

If any of you kids are reading this, I want you to strengthen your mind and stand up to take responsibility of your lives. Step forward to make that positive change, take an interest in your future, and have a passion for the goodness of life. Start by speaking to your school's guidance counselors and searching the internet for whatever it is that interests you. Your school's guidance counselors are there for you. They are the ones who can help and guide you on the path toward your future. I've only given you a handful of ideas. However, there are thousands of career choices that will suit your personalities. There are people who are willing to help you, but you have to be willing to meet them halfway. And do know that your road to success will not be easy, and you will make mistakes. That's just the way it is. Stand back up, learn from your mistakes, and try always to have back-up plans A, B, C, D, and E. You can make that dream of being whatever you want a reality. Believe in yourself, and just do it. What my grandfather shared with me, I will share with you: "A dream is wishful thinking; a goal is a dream with a plan and a deadline." May God bless our school kids.

All in a Day's Work

SITUATIONS THAT SOME might consider ridiculous, strange, unbelievable, outrageous, or low-down dirty are everyday, normal life for me and my coworkers. My first experiences on the vehicles—with baby mama dramas, human waste, altercations over the fare, vehicle breakdowns, verbal threats and abuse, smoking, people having seizures, and thrown objects—made me frustrated and angry, gave me the creeps, caused headaches and made me sick, had me sweating, and made me think I was hallucinating. Every person I looked at turned into a demon.

But I learned to concentrate on my well being and to accept that this behavior is normal to many riders. Today, nothing that occurs on my vehicle fazes me because I expect the chaos. When I do get frustrated, it is because I am tired of all the stupidity aboard my vehicle. I have certainly experienced such shocking things that when I tell my stories, people accuse me of lying. If the situations were reversed, it would be hard for me to believe them too. But the fact of the matter is, I am telling the truth. I could not make this up.

When I am behind that wheel, nothing anyone can say or do surprises me. I have experienced practically every evil that could be cast upon man. I said "practically" because I have yet to experience having a weapon pointed at my head, being robbed or raped, or seeing anyone having sexual intercourse aboard my vehicle. The only thing I can do is pray every day for my safety, hope for a blessed day, and shake my head at the foolishness. Sometimes I believe that I am on another planet because my day at work is so strikingly unimaginable. I certainly have had my share of the most provocative, unpleasant, bizarre, and difficult situations. From the frustrations of management to the insane behavior of the public, it is all in a day's work. I expect foolishness from the public and unethical behavior from management.

There is nothing special or different about my job. It is just the same, old routine day after day. I cannot stress enough how much I appreciate the many news stories on assaults on mass transit operators. However management needs to be exposed too. Given the many projects that the transit authority has been and is involved with, when will it begin the project to develop more restrooms for operators at the end of the transit line? No, not portable potties, but actual restrooms. And when will the transit authority fix the few restrooms that operators do have, after weeks and months of being out of service? This brings me to story time.

What About Us?

I'd just reached the end of the transit line and had to use the restroom badly. For some reason, the key that the transit authority provided to me would not unlock the restroom door. Four of my coworkers noticed me jumping up and down and shaking like a drug addict going through withdrawal; they tried their keys and still the door did not open. Holding my breath and squeezing my legs together, I walked lopsided to my vehicle and hopped up the steps. I pushed the button to connect with HQ, explained the problem, and asked them to please send a supervisor. Headquarters asked, "Can't you use the restroom at the restaurant or supermarket down the street?" I replied in a fast and loud voice, "No! I'm not gonna make it! The restaurant is closed and the market is too far." I was stunned and felt insulted. After I give the details about my situation, you question me instead of sending a supervisor? I'm a grown person, not a child. I know how to ask to use a restroom.

After about two minutes I could no longer wait for a supervisor. I called headquarters to say that I was out of service and returning to the depot. Then I called my depot on my cell phone and explained my case to the dispatcher there, adding, "I peed on myself." As I walked into the depot humiliated, wet, and smelling like a hot, rotten cantaloupe, the dispatcher said not to worry, everything had been taken care of with HQ and I could go home. The very next day at work I told a manager that our keys would not unlock the restroom door. His reply was, "That particular lock has been changed and is for the train men because the operators leave the restrooms filthy." I asked, "What train men? The regional rail guys? I don't believe that. I believe whoever is responsible doesn't give a damn about us. How could they change the locks without notifying us? Now what are we supposed to do? Walk to the market even though there is a restroom ten feet from us?" He said, "I'm sorry. The decision wasn't mine. It came from downtown." I left his office and spoke to the union reps, who did not believe that. They believed it was an in-house decision. Still, something good did come from this situation. I was secretly given a restroom key that worked and had several copies made and distributed to my coworkers.

You think my tales are over? Well, they are not. Folks, I am about to reveal a personal secret that will rock your world. When I have to use the restroom and I am backed up against the wall, just like the passengers, I relieve myself on the vehicles but in a different way. My friends wonder why I carry a backpack or a big purse to work. It is because I come prepared. Depending on which route I am driving and the amount of hours I am working, I'll bring any or all the household items on this list: several squeeze bottles of water, baby wipes, a bar of soap, disposable plastic gloves, a few trash bags, hand sanitizer, and always a big can of Lysol. I pop that parking brake, walk to the back of my vehicle, squat, fill the bag up, dispose it, spray, hop into my seat, pull up to the transit stop, smile, and let my people on. I am relieved and feel great. My passengers are like, "Damn, it smells good on here! What perfume you got on?" Squatting on the job is only my last resort. If there are stores, bars, malls, restaurants, or homes of family or friends along my route, I stop and I use their restrooms and have done so plenty of times. After that embarrassing incident, I promised myself that I would never be in a position like that again.

There are five-hundred-plus operators who work in my depot. Most of us have vehicles of our own. There are four rows of parking spaces available for our personal vehicles that stretch approximately between a quarter and a half of a mile. Once the parking lot is full, the only other available spaces are the ones we create. We park in the wilderness; near the back of the lot in the gravel where the trashed, old, beat-up, damaged vehicles are stored; curbside, and along the islands. The gravel consists of hard, car-tire flattening rocks with seven-inch-deep potholes where the homeless sleep and wild dogs' prowl. When it rains, the gravel is the worst place to park the vehicles. It is full of weeds, puddles of water, and tons of mud. It resembles a swamp infested with bugs, venomous snakes, and man-eating alligators. You definitely have to watch where you are walking or you will bust your ass.

My coworkers and I have asked management many times over the years if they could transform the gravel and shave down the hills that closely surround the depot and provide more parking spaces. Management, however, claims the land does not belong to the transit system. Yet when operators park curbside or along the islands because there are no available parking spaces, they have the nerve to ticket our vehicles with warning notices, penalties, and fines. Years of complaints to management and meetings with union representatives have been ignored. Wait a minute, that's not true. Part of the hilly graveled land was leveled out smoothly and evenly. But instead of providing additional parking spaces, they gave us K-9 units to sniff out hazardous materials. That's all good, fine, and dandy because safety is important and there is plenty of land available. But I want to park closer to my job. Sometimes I am so exhausted when I get off from work I want to pass out. But then I have to walk almost half a mile in the scorching sun or freezing arctic weather? One thing management never forgets about: they make sure that the overpriced candy and soda machines in the depot are full. But what about the human employees, the operators who keep this city from crumbling, who keep making money for the city? Must I remind you of what will happen if the operators are out of work? Eighty-five to 90 percent of the city will not survive. It will collapse. Whether the businesses are small or large will not matter. Money will be lost everywhere, especially at major intersections where buses and trains connect. What is the transit system's problem with showing us respect? Without the loyal employees managers would not have the Benjamins that they make.

At least I know that I would not have this job and reap all the benefits that I deserve if the transit system had not hired me. For that, I am very much appreciative and do respect the authority's positions. Why can't the respect be reciprocated? I guess the transit authority has made it clear that the dogs are more deserving of the land than are the employees who need parking spaces. Management's mistreatment of and disrespect toward the employees is inexcusable. For twenty years, there have been continual problems: passenger assaults, safety concerns, obnoxious school kids, restroom problems, lunch-break issues, mismanagement of the pension funds of 5,500 employees, and the transit system's attempts to take back the benefits that the employees have battled long and hard to secure. I thought the goal of the mass transit was to display a positive image. How can it be positive when most of the employees are constantly being beat down and stomped on by our employer?

The governor had to intervene over a contract between the transit authority and the employees' local union. The transit authority wanted to eliminate the no-layoff clause, which stated that once an employee has one year on the job, he or she cannot be laid off. When I started working there, I prayed, begged, and hoped every day that we did not strike or that management did not need to cut back on labor. I counted down the months, weeks, days, hours, and minutes; I could not wait until my year was up. If the transit authority eliminated the no-layoff clause during a recession there, would have been a civil war. You think the flash mob and winning the World Series gave this city problems? Lay-off hundreds or thousands of transit employees, and try to believe this city will be safe. There would be mass destruction. This city would be torn up beyond recognition. After the employees rampage through this city, it will look like a third world country. You might think that an earthquake, hurricane, and tornado touched down at the same time. The broadcasting stations might name it "the prelude to Armageddon."

Management also wanted to eliminate our cost of living increases, change the scheduling of our payroll from weekly to every biweekly, and change our seniority status (we chose our shifts in the order we were hired; they wanted to choose our shifts randomly). The transit authority also wanted to increase the employees' prescription plan rates, healthcare contribution rates, and the medical provider in-network deductibles. However, I am proud to announce that the employees and the union stood as one, an unbreakable force of power, and won. We retained our past gains and current rights. It was all in a day's work.

There have been so many stories in the media about this, and those who are unaware of our circumstances are constantly asking me if what we are fighting for is really worth the fuss. I respond with a "hell, yeah, of course it is." And when I have the time to explain, I'll say, "When management tries to take away your standards of living and makes conditions practically unbearable for the employees, as the last resort, a strike is always necessary." It is a funny thing; when outsiders hear about contract negotiations or a possible strike, the only thing that comes to their minds is money. The media do not list all the contract issues to be negotiated; then again the few that are listed cause the public to lash out at transit operators. Throughout the city, you can hear the phrase "Y'all make a lot of damn money as it is, and ya'll got the nerve to strike for more? Greedy bastards! What y'all need to do is stop breaking down and run on time!" Then when details about the last day of negotiations hits the airwaves and the president of the union lays the issues on the table, desperately trying to prevent a strike, the public sings a different tune. Now all of a sudden they understand our hardship. They start worrying that there really might be a strike at midnight.

I believe a good portion of the people do not know or understand what the purpose of a labor union is. It is an organization of employees who represent and pursue the rights of their coworkers to maintain or improve everyday working conditions. The mass transit system authority employee contract issues deal with more than just money. There are a host of items that union representatives negotiate with management. The topics of these negotiations include the employees' working environment, safety issues, job functions, complaint processing, benefits, policies, etc. Unions are important because not only do they fight for your rights, they enable employees 24/7 to address any concerns comfortably and privately if needed.

I want members of the public to understand that I am not personally attacking their characters, only their actions. And don't any of you transit riders front because you know exactly what I am talking about. You either witness the problems or are part of them. Writing this memoir has made me feel like I am writing a movie script for a horror, adventure, or fantasy movie. But these are real-life actions taking place on planet Earth with real people on public vehicles. If I go five minutes into my workday without any commotion, I will be lying in the hospital with a heart attack. On my job that rarely happens. Somebody will get on my vehicle without any money, eating a cheese steak, or with a loaded shopping cart blocking the aisle. The transit authority needs to fund programs and establish TV stations about transit workers. They need to equip *all* buses with functional cameras. The public must understand the importance of keeping the operators' sanity in check. The public must understand that we need to concentrate. They need to be educated on the rules and regulations and the reasons for them. They need to be taught etiquette. They need to know that transit vehicles break down just like personal vehicles do. They need to know that they will go to prison if they assault a transit employee.

This should be a transit-authority-funded project to develop such commercials and educational programs. Will this happen within the next year or two? I highly doubt it. Anything that has to do with employee issues usually gets overlooked. The worst thing about this is that a great number of the managers were once operators. My, my, my; once they are promoted, how soon they forget where they came from. They turn their backs on us, shit on us, and try to flush us down the toilet. Operators are worn out and need to see immediate improvements. There simply is not enough protection from gross and violent encounters, such as someone spitting on you, throwing a drink at you, and yelling in your ear, which the baby mamas are particularly good at. To tell you the truth, I absolutely hate dealing with women and their baby strollers. Yes, I said hate, and I know exactly what it means. I despise having to pick up some of them. And it is not only the teenagers and young mothers; some of these baby mamas are full-blown grown women. After I tell them it is for the protection of the child, would you believe they snap back with, "Whatever! I'm only going a few blocks anyway." And they will not shut up, repeating all of the injuries they would love to inflict on me as well as insults until they get off. With their fire-cracker attitudes they are ready to draw blood. When they open their mouths, bundles of ignorance pours out. In just about every baby-mama-drama altercation, I want to say, "Bitch! I ain't none of your babies' daddies! You had better call them if you know them"! For some reason these baby mamas cannot accept me giving them a direct order. When their behavior and language becomes unbearable, I call the police to escort them and their children off my vehicle before continuing in service. And, yes, I have put both mother and child off my vehicle in bad weather conditions. I refuse to drive distressed. I feel sorry for the baby, but not the baby mamas. They have to know that they cannot drag a stroller that is equivalent to a refrigerator onto a mass transit vehicle.

Lord forbid, there were an emergency evacuation. During such crises, people get nervous; they may cause a stampede, fall, get stuck or tangled; and there is a high possibility that a child in a stroller could get seriously injured. In addition, strollers could hurt passengers by blocking the aisles. My child is a gift from God Almighty, the most valuable, precious, joyous, and irreplaceable present that I could ever receive. If I get any helpful information and procedures about how to protect my child, I am always willing to listen and learn. Just follow directions! Why is that so difficult? If you are riding on public transportation the safest position for an infant is in the comfort of a person's arms. That is not to say that a held child cannot be injured but probably not to the extreme where there is major damage. Neither myself nor my coworkers want a child to be involved in an accident on our watch.

There is no need to take a trip to a zoo or a safari. If entertainment is what you are searching for, we got it. If you are in need of a brain shocker or want to double over in laughter, we can do that too. You want to see a fashion show called "I Know She Didn't Come Out of the House Looking Like That"; the real dirty dancers, and dog-howling singers? Join me aboard the mass transit vehicles, where all this live entertainment of jungle bunnies and circus freaks are under one roof. There is no limit to the action, and best of all, you can get it all for just $2.00!

I can recall the very first time that I experienced one of these shows. It was a Friday after midnight with a few men aboard. I drove a few blocks and then picked up a gang of men. As they entered the vehicle they spoke to and made several comments about me. As always, I kept a pleasant yet blank expression and said, "Thanks," nothing more. However, a few of the men who sat in the front seats seemed to be unsatisfied with this; they muttered among themselves and stared at me. They growled about my body and asked dumb questions. Instantly, I got an uneasy feeling. I became so uptight that I began silently praying to the Lord, like someone begging for her life: "My gracious God, Lord Heavenly Father who is my Savior, please just this once please, I like everything and unconditionally love everybody. I will be good, stop drinking, and go to church three times a week

Oh, Lord God, even if you could just power me up and turn me into the bionic woman right here, right now so I could shred their asses up like chewing tobacco, I won't do it. Lord, please save my life! I don't want to let loose." I held on to my prayer before saying amen. I felt the comfort in this.

I pulled over at the next stop and thought my vision was playing tricks on me. I opened the doors and sure enough a young girl in her teens or early twenties, standing about five foot six with a body like Pinky the porn star entered my vehicle. She had a rhinestone handbag, matching sandals, and a sultry pink and red lace bra and panties lingerie set. My facial expression screamed, "What the fuck? You dizzy ho! Do you know what you just got 'us' into?" And I thought, *I did ask the lord to remove me from this situation and while I do not go to church, I do have some religion. And I know this here is not the work of the Lord.* The most terrifying moment during my first year as a big city transit driver could not have come at a more sinister time. Again I asked quietly, "Lord, is this all because I said 'ass'? The word "ass" is in the Holy Bible. Please don't punish me, Lord. I didn't mean it. I'm sorry, Lord. Please bless my soul and forgive me."

Trying to warn her, I widened my eyes, giving her this crazed look and shaking my head at a fast pace. Then it hit me, *She ain't gonna listen to you. She's crazy her damn self.* And the men screamed when they saw her. They were in la-la land. The men that had been taunting me were now slobbering over her. With a teasing smile across her face, she walked slowly to the middle of the vehicle, turned her butt to face the rear of the vehicle, where most of the men were, bent over, and booty clapped. The men lost their minds. They went ballistic. As my great-grandmother used to say, "They were more excited than a gay man with a bag of dicks." They were interested in more action. She sat on one guy's lap, allowed him and others to rub on her, engaged in sexual conversations, and was offered money for blow jobs. Then a man shouted, "Yo, cutie behind the wheel, come back here and give "Glazed Doughnut" a run for her money." The men broke out in loud laughter and began slapping hands in agreement. After that, I knew it was all over for me. I was about to be a victim of rape.

Then a man said, "I would love to see that shit, but damn! Of all nights, I gots to be somewhere tonight. Yo, record this shit." He walked toward the front doors. But before he exited he asked me, "You do this route every night?" Opening the doors, I replied, "No." He blew a kiss my way and then said, "You're a cute ass. I'ma see you again for sure." I said to myself, *for sure* What was that supposed to mean? He was going to stalk me? He was going to do some freaky shit or expect, perhaps force, me to do something against my will? Anyhow, since Glazed Doughnut was taking much of the attention away from me, I turned on the four-way blinkers, stopped in the middle of the street, gathered my belongings, glided out of my seat, and got my scarred ass off that vehicle. Yes, with the passengers aboard, I abandoned the vehicle and began fumbling with my phone, trying to dial 911. Nervous, running and walking, hoping to flag down a cop, I heard a guy behind me yelling several times, "Miss, where you going?"

Panicking, I pulled out my pocket knife, turned toward him, and began slashing the air and screaming, "Get away from me!" As he was dodging me, he waved his badge and shouted twice, "I'm a cop! I'm not going to hurt you. Could you please put the knife away? Are you okay?"

Still excited, but slightly relieved and at the same time trying to catch my breath, I put the knife away and said to the officer, "You're joking. Were you on that vehicle? And if not, did I just try to kill you?" He laughed a little and asked, "Can I just ask you a question? Where are you going? I mean, aren't you the driver?" I replied, "Yeah, I'm the driver and so what? Fuck everybody on that vehicle, I'm going home. Tonight is my last night, meaning y'all are on your own. You and none of those assholes on that vehicle are going to force me into an orgy!" The way he laughed, you would have thought that I was a comedian. He replied, still laughing and sucking his teeth, "They're just talking shit. They're not going to do anything to you. Everybody is standing outside the vehicle wondering where you went. And that chic got off and walked down the street. If it makes you feel any better, there's another cop on the vehicle and we're not going to let anyone hurt you." I was still on edge but felt some comfort and agreed to return to the vehicle. A few of the passengers standing outside asked if I were okay and stated that they were only having a little fun and meant me no harm. I drove off, the men left me alone, there were no more problems, and I said, "Thank you, Lord, amen."

Later, my mother and a few coworkers asked me, "Why you

didn't call headquarters?" I answered, "I panicked." Believe me, I thought about calling HQ but that was not the first thing to come across my mind. And I was thinking about saving my life. I thought it might be too late by the time a supervisor or a cop reached me. I thought about what might happen if help did come? They'll remove the girl and maybe a few men, but then again, I'll be left alone. Who's to say that the men who remain on the vehicle won't try to do anything to me after the help leaves? Who's to say those men who were put off won't wait for me to come back around? You know that type of stuff happens, right? But the main thing that I was praying and thinking about was my life: *Please don't rape me. I don't want to be a victim of a gangbang*. I thought that was the most outrageous and awkward situation that I could ever be in. I even thought that I was the first operator to experience as anything like that.

Boy was I wrong. I found out that after midnight on this particular route, female passengers modeling their lingerie line is the norm. There is definitely no shame in their game. They are actually working or going to work. They constantly ride up and down on my vehicle to pull trick after trick with different men who meet them at the transit stops. So, yes, I have had my share of assorted dramas. A few make me laugh, some give me headaches, and others make me want to shoot someone dead. In this next story, a few people had different reactions but for the most part people cracked the hell up, and I was one of them. As absurd as the situation was, it made me laugh so hard that I was crying, because

I truly could not believe that people actually do this crap in public and, worse, in broad daylight.

I pulled over at a transit stop, and another operator relieved me. I stayed on about five minutes so I could go to a particular store. On my return trip, I jumped on another bus and stood in the middle, holding on to the bars. A couple of seconds later, out of nowhere, a man in his late thirties to mid-forties, wearing a snap-on sweat suit, similar to the ones professional basketball players wear, began dancing and repeatedly and loudly singing the chorus of Nelly's song: "It's getting hot in here, whaaat, so take off all your clothes. I am getting so hot, I wanna take my clothes off." The next thing this fool did made me scream, "Oh, my God!" He snatched that sweat suit off and was penis and ass naked! The people aboard were horrified. People stood on their seats and tried to move away from him. Some were laughing while others covered their mouths with their hands in total disbelief. The remarks people made did not faze this man. He continued to dance hard while his dick flipped, flopped, and flapped everywhere. He reminded me of how Martin Lawrence danced on the *Martin* show.

By the time the female operator pulled over to the stop where I got off, the male passengers had about all they could take from this clown. When the operator opened the back doors, these guys all at once kicked his naked ass off of the vehicle and threw his clothes behind him. Stumbling as he got up, he strolled his nakedness down the street, dressing himself. I can speak for me that that surely was the last striptease dance aboard MT that I had ever seen. Other men have flashed me but not while they were butt-naked and dancing.

This next incident was definitely my first and last; however it occurs more often than you'd think to many of my coworkers. During my teenage years the most deviant thing that kids did during "mischief night," better known as "mystery night," was to throw eggs at parked vehicles and homes. I will never forget the next morning, Halloween (my favorite time of the year), opening the front door with the morning air smelling like sewage and the neighborhood cars covered in dried egg yolks and shells. All of the neighbors would be outside, cussing and swearing about what they would do if they caught a kid vandalizing their vehicles. Nowadays it is not only eggs being thrown or only the kids behaving badly during mystery night. When adults get involved, there is no more egg throwing. These immature, jealous, and poisonous adults will carve the metal out of vehicles, flatten tires, and place dog poop under door handles. You how I know this? It is because these idiots— friends of friends or family, coworkers, neighbors, and acquaintances—talk about it. I try my hardest to distance myself from these gossip junkies who enjoy trouble.

This was my nightmare on mass transit. It was mystery night, and there were a handful of people sitting on the bus. The ride is okay until I reach a certain section of the city, the hood, a rough-looking neighborhood where hoodlums dwell. The hood is also where the passengers, my vehicle and I experience all of the mischievous activities. In addition to the egg throwing, there are rocks, bricks, frozen soda bottles, and frozen eggs. Windows get shattered, other things get dents, and worst of all when people are boarding or exiting the vehicle, we all become targets. The fumes were so disgusting it reminded me of a pigpen. I had to pull my vehicle over and spray my can of Lysol, and then drive with my window open. I knew I was not supposed to spray with passengers aboard my vehicle, but damn it, it stunk. I'll tell you one thing, my passengers didn't complain. They appreciated it. My shift was coming to an end, and I believed my shift ended between 7:45 p.m. and 8:15 p.m. Three tall, slender men were waiting at the end of the line. I stood up and stretched my arms and legs as the passengers exited the vehicle. One of them mentioned something about mystery night and told me to be safe.

As soon as that passenger stepped off the vehicle, one of the three guys approached my front doors to ask me a question. I told him, "I'm out of service." As I leaned over to grab the handle to shut my doors, a little voice inside of me said, *Don't sit down, and keep your eyes on those guys*. I looked at them and saw this guy take the lid off this huge plastic container filled with liquid, which he threw toward me. I quickly jumped back. There are absolutely no words to explain how I felt at that moment. All I know is, I was an emotional wreck and felt yucky. Luckily the doors shut before the jerk could throw the full container of animal or human waste on me. I had to walk to the back of the vehicle because of the toxic fumes of the urine and feces. I began checking my clothing and rubbing my head to make sure nothing got on me. My body felt so weak, I was bent over, gagging, trying to throw up, but nothing never came out of my mouth but globs of spit. After getting myself together, I grabbed a few loose papers to cover the waste. I carefully examined my area and covered my seat with paper. If my seat made the paper wet that vehicle would have sat in that spot until help arrived. After about ten minutes, I was ready to bring this slop into the depot. As I started the ignition, the punks reappeared and threw two more containers of waste on the windshields and the front doors, then ran off laughing.

If I'd had a gun in my possession, today I would be spending the rest of my life in prison with three consecutive life sentences, possibly death row, convicted of murder. Often I sit back and say to myself, *I really understand why operators are not allowed to bear weapons*. Can you imagine how many homicides they would commit? Instead of being listed as one of the top-ten biggest cities in the United States, this city would be listed as one of the smallest villages. The focus would no longer be on the public's abuse on operators; instead, it would be about the operators' massacres of the passengers. For sure, I would be one of those passengers' worst nightmare—forget Freddy Kruger! I would butcher every potential threat without hesitation, cutting, slicing, slashing, shooting, running people over and off the road! Once the public finally saw who I am, their reaction would be, "Shorty? You're the one talking all this big stuff?" Yeah, I am five feet, four inches tall. But do not underestimate me because, babe, I can roll with the best of ya! I am sure there are a lot of *Star Wars* fans reading my memoir. Well, remember Jedi Master Yoda, the green dwarf who defeated Dooku (the former Jedi Master and now Dark Lord of the Sith) in *Stars Wars Episode II: The Attack of the Clones*? That duel was awesome! For years, I have always wondered what made Yoda this kingly Jedi Master. Finally I have seen Yoda's fighting skills challenged by someone with equivalent combative skills. Impressed? I was astounded! I never would have imagined that an old, two-foot-tall dwarf who had a limp and a cane and could barely walk, close to one thousand years old would have such supreme speed and acrobatic skills. In the fighting scene, I especially loved this particular part when Yoda blocked Dooku's lightning force so diligently with the palm of his hand and said, "Much to learn, you still have." The whole movie theater jumped up, gave a standing ovation, and screamed, "Ooh, shit! Kick his ass, Yoda!" The grandeur of that moment was magical. With that, you can call me Yoda.

When I pulled into the vault lane, where the transit employees take certain mandatory information, they held their noses, waved at me to continue driving through, and yelled, "Don't come back through here. Park it." I did exactly that and could not get home fast enough. Once I was through my doors, I was so determined to take off my work clothes that I busted every button off my shirt and threw my top, pants, and sweater in the trash outside and covered them in bleach. I stayed in the shower for two hours. I felt slimy. I washed over, under, and in-between every crack in my body. Usually, I would snack on some cake or fruit before going to bed. I could not bring myself to eat anything. For the rest of that week I could not eat breakfast, brunch, lunch, a snack, junk food, dinner, or dessert. The thought of food made me want to barf.

Not wanting to eat is a rare and an extremely unusual condition for me because my passion is enjoying good food. I absolutely love to eat. If you believe this type of gruesome and disturbed act does not come about often or would never happen to you, do not become a mass transit operator. We are not provided with protective shields, and everything, including our lives, is fair game behind the wheel.

My family and friends have told me that working with the public is the worst job to have. I have been told by hundreds of passengers what they would rather do than my job. A few of my favorites are:

1. I'd rather smell musty arm pits than do your job. (I would faint.)
2. I'd rather clean up poop all day than do your job. (I would puke.)
3. I'd rather sit in a snake pit than do your job, (I hope they're garden snakes.)
4. I'd rather have a toothache than do your job. (This quote belongs to my uncle—smile!)
5. I'd rather be chased by bees than do your job. (You can't run forever.)
6. I'd rather try to outrun an avalanche than do your job. (I'll be at your funeral.)
7. I'd rather be Satan's dog than do your job or try to make anyone like me for that matter. (This quote belongs to my dear grandmom—love ya!)

Better you than me. I'd rather continue being an operator than do anything from that list. I do like my job and enjoy being around people. I chose this job because I really do enjoy driving. Once I get into my zone, I am at ease, comfortable, and relaxed. Most of my rides are smooth and easygoing. I take interest in the scenery, the restaurants, malls, theaters, museums, and in just viewing other sections of the city. Finding different directions or short cuts to get to certain locations has made my personal commutes easier. I love working outside than being cooped up in an office. I know my supervisors are driving around, but I mainly love the fact that there is no one standing over my shoulders every other minute. Written complaints come in every now and then, but hey, that's all in a day's work. And hallelujah, I do not have to work around backstabbers and brownnosers (they're pathetic) all day. When I am on my vehicle I am alone, all by myself. Being able to curb my anger and frustrations has enabled me to grow into a better human being. I have come to see that angry folk are mainly angry by themselves and have learned how to ease my way through strenuous situations without tempers flaring. When I am behind that wheel, I always find the inner peace and happiness I need to get me through the day. Just being in the mix of everyday life has always been fascinating to me. That is what living is all about.